KW-484-934

The Tottenham Hotspur Story

TOTTENHAM HOTSPUR FOOTBALL CLUB

Founded: 1882
Colours: White Shirts, Dark Blue Shorts
Ground: White Hart Lane, Tottenham, London N 17
Telephone: 01-801-6451
Ground capacity: 52,000
Record Attendance: 75,038 v Sunderland, FA Cup 6th Rd 5 March 1938
Record Receipts: £49,920 v Feyenoord UEFA Cup Final (1st leg), 21 May 1974
Pitch measurement: 110 yards by 73 yards
Honours: First Division Champions 1950-1, 1960-1: runners-up 1921-2. 1951-2, 1956-7, 1962-3. Second Division Champions: 1919-20, 1949-50: runners-up 1908-09, 1932-3. Promoted as third club 1977-8 FA Cup Winners: 1901 (as a Non-League club), 1921, 1961, 1962, 1967. Football League Cup winners: 1971, 1973. European Cup-winners Cup holders 1963. UEFA Cup winners 1972; runners-up 1974.
Record Win: 13-2 v Crewe Alex FA Cup 4th Rd. Replay, 3 February 1960
Record Defeat: 0-7 v Liverpool, First Division, 2 September 1978
Most League Points gained: 70, Division Two, 1919-20
Most League Goals scored: 115, First Division, 1960-1
Highest League scorer in a season: Jimmy Greaves, 37 in 1962-3
Most League appearances: Pat Jennings 472 from 1964 to 1977
Managers since World War II: Joe Hulme, Arthur Rowe, Jimmy Anderson, Bill Nicholson, Terry Neill, Keith Burkinshaw
How to reach White Hart Lane: Underground to Manor House (on Piccadilly line) or Seven Sisters (Victoria line). From Manor House, buses 259 and 279; from Seven Sisters, buses 67, 149, 171, 243, 259, 123, 279. White Hart Lane station is served from Liverpool Street and is three minutes walk from the ground.
Address of Supporters club: 744 High Road, Tottenham, London N 17

The
TOTTENHAM HOTSPUR
Story

Anton Rippon

Moorland Publishing

Picture Sources. Illustrations have been provided by:
BBC Hulton Picture Library: 10, 12; Central Press
Photos: 25, 27-9, 33-5, 38, 40, 42, 44, 45, 48, 49 (RHS), 50,
53, 55, 59, 61, 63-4, 68-9, 73, 77, 79, 81, 83, 86, 88, 90,
95 (bottom LHS); Colorsport: 11, 14-16, 18-22, 24, 26,
30-2, 36-7, 39, 41, 43, 46-7, 49 (LHS), 51-2, 54, 56-8, 60,
62, 65-7, 76, 82, 85, 93-4, 95 (except bottom LHS);
Sporting Pictures (UK): 91.

ISBN 0 903485 97 4

© Anton Rippon 1980

All rights reserved. No part of this publication may be
reproduced, stored in a retrieval system, or transmitted in
any form or by any means, electronic, mechanical,
photocopying, recording or otherwise, without the prior
permission of Moorland Publishing Company Ltd.

Typeset by Alacrity Phototypesetters,
Banwell Castle, Weston-super-Mare, Avon
and printed in Great Britain by
Redwood Burn Ltd, Trowbridge & Esher
for Moorland Publishing Co Ltd,
PO Box 2, Ashbourne, Derbyshire DE6 1DZ

1882-1950

THE BEGINNINGS

The schoolboys who formed a football team in London's Northumberland Park area in 1882 showed vivid imagination when they called their team Hotspur FC after one of the most romantic figures in English history. Harry Hotspur, son of the first Earl of Northumberland, had a reputation as a bold and fierce warrior and he was eventually immortalised by William Shakespeare. But even those imaginative nineteenth-century schoolboys could not have foreseen what romantic deeds their own club would achieve over the next hundred years. In that age of gas lamps and horse-drawn trams, they would have no idea that their small club would grow to become one of the most famous in the world, striding across the Continent to do battle in the soccer capitals of Europe. Even so, Tottenham Hotspur was to achieve prominence fairly rapidly. Within twenty years they would become the first southern professional club to win the FA Cup — and they would do so before the world's largest football attendance of 114,815 which still stands as the third largest ever to see a football match in England.

The boys who founded Tottenham Hotspur Football Club were already members of a cricket team of the same name. Legend has it that the football section was born under a lamp post in Tottenham High Road, just a stone's throw from the original family home of the Earl of Northumberland whose son's name was adopted by the local schoolboy sportsmen. The boys themselves came from the Northumberland Avenue — the road which connects Tottenham High Road with Tottenham Marshes, and it was the Marshes which provided a convenient answer to the problem of where to play. Those early Spurs simply staked a claim on Saturday afternoons by marking out a pitch and erecting goalposts with tape for a crossbar. The site of Spurs first pitch can still be found by crossing the railway at Northumberland Park station and following the road to the right towards the northern end of the Marshes, although today the site is overshadowed by industry and is far removed from the open spaces where the youngest Spurs played almost a century ago.

The drawback to the unofficial method of reserving a pitch was that it was open to abuse and older and bigger boys would just push the young Spurs off the ground they had so lovingly prepared. Spurs soon solved the problem. At the start of their second season in 1883, the boys enlisted the help of some adults from the Tottenham Parish Church of All Hallows where some of them attended Bible classes. One of the men who answered their call for help was John Ripsher, a Bible class teacher at the church. Immediately, Ripsher became president and treasurer of Hotspur FC and found the club headquarters at the local YMCA in Percy House. Strangely, Percy House stood on the site of a former family home of the Earl of Northumberland and the connecting thread with the Hotspur club and the family of its legendary hero was maintained.

That second season was a successful one for Spurs. They won nine of their eleven games and scored thirty-two goals, although a local 'derby' match with Edmonton club Latymer drew criticism in the local Press of 'coarse remarks' by some of the spectators — an embarrassing charge to be levelled at a club deeply involved with the local church. Of course, there was little the club could do because the Marshes were open and spectators had a free view and were subject to no control from the teams they chose to support.

In 1884-5, Hotspur FC became officially known as Tottenham Hotspur, basically because there was another club called London Hotspur. Tottenham Hotspur won eighteen of their twenty-eight matches in their first season under the name which was to ring out across the world in years to come, and on 4 April 1885, the club cancelled its match so that the players might go to Kennington Oval to see Blackburn Rovers win the FA Cup Final by beating Queen's Park, the famous Scottish amateurs. Spurs were so impressed by the Lancashire club that they decided to adopt Blackburn's famous blue and white shirts.

> *Spurs team to play St Albans in their first-ever competitive match in October 1885 was:*
> *T. Bumberry; J. Jull, W. Tyrell; H. Casey, F. Lovis, H. Bull; R. Amos, F. Cottrell, W. Mason, W. Harston, R. Buckle.*

On 17 October 1885, in their fourth season, Tottenham Hotspur played their first-ever competitive match when a London business house team called St Albans visited Tottenham Marshes in the first round of the London FA Cup. Tottenham won 5-2 before 400 spectators and playing at inside-left that day was Billy Harston, still a frequent visitor to White Hart Lane in the 1950s. The next round proved well beyond the capabilities of the young

Spurs. They had to travel to Wandsworth to play the famous public school and universities team Casuals and lost 8-0. But that defeat apart, it was another good season for Tottenham Hotspur with twenty-four wins in thirty-seven matches.

In 1886-7 Spurs reached the final of the East End Cup and only a fluke goal by Caledonians, which skidded across a rain-sodden Marshes pitch and through the legs of a luckless Spurs goalkeeper, John Anderson, decided the match. During the season Tottenham changed their dressing rooms from Somerford Grove to the Milford — although from either they faced a mile-long walk to the pitch!

Spurs sixth season in 1887-8, when they were boosted by some older players from the recently disbanded men's team Park FC, saw the first of what is today Tottenham's traditional 'derby' match against Arsenal. Arsenal were then Royal Arsenal and played south of the Thames at Plumstead, long before they moved to Highbury to become Spurs' arch-rivals in North London. Royal Arsenal scored first in this inaugural fixture but Spurs were soon 2-1 ahead and only some brave goalkeeping by Arsenal's Beardsley, recently signed from Nottingham Forest, prevented Tottenham from increasing their lead. The match was abandoned with a quarter-of-an-hour to play when darkness made it impossible to continue. But Spurs had done enough to establish themselves as one of London's leading clubs.

Success brought problems, not least problems of crowd control. For six seasons as Tottenham Hotspur had grown in stature, spectators had enjoyed a free view of the club's successes. Secretary Frank Hatton, who had taken over when he joined the club from Park FC, was among those committee members who pushed hard for Tottenham Hotspur to seek a new home, one where they could charge for admission and capitalise on the hundreds of supporters they now had. At the end of 1887-8 Tottenham Hotspur found a new ground not far from their present home at White Hart Lane. Officials negotiated the tenancy of a field behind a nursery in Northumberland Park. It was a significant move. Ground improvements meant that paying spectators could be accomodated and Spurs were well on the way to becoming one of the South's premier clubs.

Spurs charged sixpence admission to see their match with Old Etonians on 13 October 1888. Six years earlier, while Spurs were being formed, Old Etonians were winning the FA Cup. Spurs team when the two sides met in the London Senior Cup in the 1888-9 season was: G. Baldock, J. Jull, A. Crossley; H. Bull, H. Casey, W. Tyrell; F. Cottrell, W. Mason, T. Purdie, W. Harston, R. Buckle.

In 1888-9 came the match that confirmed Spurs' status. They met Old Etonians in the first round of the London Senior Cup at Northumberland Park. Spur lost 8-2 (although they held Old Etonians 3-2 at the interval) but the result was unimportant. The real significance was that six years before, when Hotspur FC was being formed by a bunch of eager schoolboys, Old Etonians were winning the FA Cup. Now they competed in the same competitions — it was a great leap forward. That same season Tottenham's right-back and skipper, J. C. Jull, was chosen to play for Middlesex. He was the first of a long line of Spurs players who would win representative honours with a host of countries and organisations.

Tottenham Hotspur became members of the Football Association in 1888-9 when the club's annual balance in hand was just £61.

Spurs fixture list became stronger and stronger. In 1889-90 (the players were still expected to pay 7s 6d annual subscription at that time), matches were arranged against Arsenal, Swindon Town, Luton Town and Clapton, although there were some red faces in the Spurs dressing room on the opening day of the season when Arsenal beat them 10-1 at Plumstead. But that blemish was soon put behind them and the following season, Tottenham enjoyed success in the London Senior Cup. They beat Queen's Park Rangers, Barking and Barnes before losing to Millwall Athletic — later Millwall FC of the Football League. The season had seen the emergence of a new centre-half in the shape of Stan Briggs, a man who was to serve Tottenham well for many years to come.

In 1892-3 competitive league football came to Spurs ground at Northumberland Park when they became founder members of the newly-formed Southern Alliance, joining Old St Stephen's, Erith, Windsor and Eton and Upton Park. It was another good move. Spurs finished the season, winning seven and drawing two of their twelve league games and enjoying an unbeaten home record. J. C. Jull was still playing regularly and Billy Harston was also turning out. In the London Senior Cup, Spurs reached the fourth round before losing 1-0 to Casuals in front of a record gate of 3,000 at Northumberland Park. At sixpence a time, the takings amounted to £75. Spurs also entered the Wolverton Charity Cup and reached the semi-final before the Birmingham team Smethwick beat them 2-0.

The crowd record at Northumberland Park was to be broken again late in the 1892-3 season when a Tottenham and District team played an Edmonton and District team for charity and over 4,000 packed into the ground. Spurs flying doctor — a physician called Sykes who was making a name for himself as a speedy winger — was chosen to play for Surrey and, all in all, Tottenham Hotspur could look back on their first season in league football with much satisfaction. Good results and booming gate receipts made it a happy time for all.

> *In 1892-3, Spurs changed their colours to red shirts and blue shorts and for a while the club was known as 'The Tottenham Reds'.*

Season 1893-4 was the season of 'the affair of Payne's boots'. In retrospect, the whole business seems rather laughable, and yet it was probably the thing which sent Tottenham Hotspur on the road to professionalism. Professionalism, while being legalised in the North and Midlands in 1885, was still frowned upon by the London Football Association. On 21 October 1893, Tottenham Hotspur offered a place to a left-winger called Ernie Payne. Although he was on the books of fellow amateurs Fulham, Payne had not been selected by that club for any matches in 1892-3 and he jumped at the chance of playing first team football with Spurs.

On the morning of his debut, Payne was issued with Tottenham Hotspur shirt, shorts and stockings, but had no football boots. His own had been somehow 'stolen' from Fulham's ground and Spurs made a grave error in giving the left-winger ten shillings to enable him to go out and buy some replacements from a nearby sports shop. Fulham were angry at the way one of their players had been allegedly poached — even though they had no use for him in their own first team — and when Fulham officials heard that the Tottenham club had given Payne money, they lodged an immediate complaint with the London Football Association. The London FA held its own inquiry which resulted in Payne being suspended for seven days and the Spurs club suspended for fourteen days. Tottenham enjoyed tremendous publicity from the Payne case and 6,000 paid to see them when they visited Southampton St Mary's some eight weeks later. The size of the crowds now willing to pay to watch football, and the experience of the Payne affair, began to open Spurs' eyes to the possibility of emulating the northern and midlands teams and adopting professionalism themselves. They knew that the London FA could not hold out in splendid isolation for ever.

In 1894 John Ripsher relinquished his position as president of Tottenham Hotspur and into his place stepped a man who would guide Spurs through to the professional ranks. John Oliver was president of the Southern Alliance in which Spurs played and his imagination was captured by the club. Oliver owned a carpet factory in London and there were always jobs for Spurs players, thus opening the door to some kind of professionalism. Soon, he had

paid for a small stand at Northumberland Park and when he became president, Oliver drove hard for Tottenham Hotspur to become a properly constituted professional club which could openly pay its players, financed by big crowds, and which could compete with the best team throughout the country. On 20 December 1895, the transformation was completed at a meeting at the Eagle public house. Bobby Buckle, a founder member of Hotspur FC in 1882, moved that Tottenham Hotspur should adopt professionalism. There was much debate. J.H. Thompson, churchwarden of All Hallows and father of two of the boys who formed the club, spoke in favour and when the vote was taken, only one hand was raised in opposition.

> *Spurs first professional side, which lost 5-0 to Stoke City in the first round of the 1895-6 FA Cup was: Ambler; Hay, Montgomery; Collins, Almond, S. Briggs; Pryor, Lanham, Hunter, Clements, Payne. Stan Briggs was entitled to his initial as the team's only amateur player – a factor that persisted into cricket right up to the 1960s.*

Immediately, the new professional players were contracted at wages ranging from fifteen shillings per week for lesser-known performers, to twenty-five shillings £1.25) per week for stars of the day. Of the amateur players, only Stan Briggs and Ernie Payne remained. The new professionals played their first FA Cup match in January 1896 when they visited Stoke City and lost 5-0. Despite the scoreline, Spurs were not disgraced. That season, Stoke were to finish sixth in a First Division won by Aston Villa. Professional Notts County beat Spurs 5-1 at Northumberland Park, but they too, were a strong side, playing Second Division football with the likes of Liverpool and Manchester City. But the Northumberland Park crowd had plenty to cheer. Arsenal were beaten 3-1 at Plumstead and Port Vale went crashing 4-0 while Middlesbrough, then the most powerful amateur side in the North of England, were crushed 5-0. Towards the end of that first

> *In 1896, FA Cup holders Aston Villa objected to Spurs' dressing room accommodation at Northumberland Avenue and hired a room at a nearby pub before beating Tottenham 3-1 before a record 6,000 crowd.*

season of professionalism, the First Division champions, Aston Villa, drew a record 6,000 spectators to Northumberland Park and won 3-1 — a creditable performance by a Spurs team against Villa who had also won the FA Cup Final at Crystal Palace the previous year.

After five seasons in the Southern Alliance, Spurs were looking to greater things. The Football League was confined mostly to clubs north of Birmingham and Leicester and the only option open to a team south of that line, who wanted to improve, was to join the Southern League which had been formed in 1894. The Southern League management committee allowed Spurs to go straight into its First Division and at the beginning of the 1896-7 season, Spurs played their first Southern League match against Sheppey United at Sheerness. Stan Briggs now captained a side which had moved from its traditional blue and white shirts, through a set of red ones, to a chocolate and gold strip. Tottenham Hotspur and Sheppey United drew 3-3 in that historic encounter and like all the moves which Spurs were making, elevation to the Southern League was yet another sensible step. They finished in fourth place. In all matches that season Spurs played sixty-seven times and won thirty, scoring 157 goals, although they conceded 108.

Most English professional teams were looking north of the border and Spurs were no exception. In 1897-8, no less than nine Scottish professionals were engaged and with Welsh international wing-half, J. L. Jones they steered the Tottenham club to third place in the Southern League's First Division. But there was a gloomier side to the Tottenham story. The club had expected even bigger attendances after turning professional but these expectations had not materialised and this began to worry committee men who were legally responsible for any debts run up by the club. To swell their coffers, the club invited famous northern teams like Sunderland and Bolton Wanderers to Northumberland Park and while these matches went some way to allay the fears of the committee, there was still precious little money to meet any sudden financial upset. At the same time the club needed cash for ground improvements and it had to find both a way to raise capital and a way to protect its members from incurring debts.

The answer was obvious. Tottenham Hotspur Football Club must become Tottenham Hotspur Football Club *Limited*. On 2 March 1898, at the Red Lion public house, it was agreed unanimously that the club should be formed into a limited company. Tottenham Hotspur Football and Athletic Company Limited was created by floating 8,000 shares at £1 each. Two of the new Board of Directors — J. H. Thompson jnr, and Robert Buckle had been players with the original Hotspur FC on Tottenham Marshes in 1882. The new Board had immediate problems. Only 1,558 of the 8,000 shares were taken up and Tottenham Hotspur slipped seventh at the end of 1898-9. In addition they had to face the fact that while Northumberland Park had been an admirable replacement for Tottenham Marshes in 1888, it was not big enough to accommodate the sort of crowds which Spurs must attract at the end of the century if they were to maintain their heady progress of the previous eighteen years.

In the history of Tottenham Hotspur, there has always been someone to assume the mantle when things have either faltered or stagnated. In 1898, two such men came along. Just as John Ripsher and John Oliver had been instrumental in helping Spurs at moments of crisis and change, so Charles Roberts and John Cameron became the men who took the club forward into the twentieth century. Roberts became chairman and Cameron took on the arduous triple role of player/manager/secretary. It was Roberts who found Tottenham Hotspur their third and final home — the now world-famous White Hart Lane. Roberts knew that thousands had risked injury when over 14,000 packed into Northumberland Avenue to see Spurs play Arsenal in an Easter holiday match. He also knew that Charringtons Brewery had just built a public house called the White Hart in Tottenham High Road — and behind the pub there was some land. The landlord of the new pub was easily persuaded but Roberts had to deal with Charringtons. They had plans to build houses on the land, thus providing a ready-made clientele for their new establishment. Roberts and his fellow director, Robert Buckle, assured the Charrington directors that the building of a football ground would bring in as much, if not more, trade than the proposed houses and with a guarantee of 1,000 minimum gates for each home match and five hundred for reserve team matches, the two Spurs directors talked the brewers round until they had a new venue for Tottenham Hotspur FC.

> *Among the names suggested for Spurs new ground were Champion Park, Gilpin Park and Percy Park. White Hart Lane was chosen because of the name of the pub on whose land the ground stood, and because White Hart Lane was the nearest railway station.*

But again there were snags. Drunkenness was a major social problem in the 1890s. Drink was cheap and was one of the few things on which the working class could spend their limited funds; in addition, there was no local licensing law and public houses could stay open all day if they so wished — and most did. All this, coupled with the commonly-held belief that football actually encouraged drunkenness, served only to scare off would-be investors in Tottenham Hotspur shares. Spurs countered the argument by saying that their team served as an example — several of the first team were total abstainers — and they found a surprising ally in the

Rev C. Sarjeant whose own football career had been cut short by injury.

Shareholders or no shareholders, Charles Roberts went ahead masterminding the move from Northumberland Park to the new ground. By midsummer 1899, the pitch had been levelled and turf laid, and the grandstand had been moved from the old ground. The new ground had seating in the dry for 2,500 and the plans show that there was accommodation for bicycles and horses on the way to the ground. The man who prepared Spurs pitch at White Hart Lane — a name chosen from several suggestions — was the same man who had prepared the wicket for the Oval Test Match against the Australians in 1880. John Over's skill in producing a playing surface far removed from the mud of the Tottenham Marshes, was as instrumental as any factor in the birth and maintenance of Spurs traditional style of skilful surface football. On 4 September 1899, Over watched Tottenham Hotspur play their first game at White Hart Lane when they beat Notts County 4-1 in a friendly match. Five thousand spectators paid £115 to begin a new era in the history of Spurs.

Just as Roberts had engineered Spurs' success off the field, so John Cameron inspired them on it. Signed at the start of the 1898-9 season, Cameron had been a talented inside-left with Queen's Park, Glasgow, and Everton. He had won caps with the Scottish international team while with the famous Glasgow club and during the close season of 1899 he set about rebuilding the Tottenham Hotspur side. Cameron signed six new players and at last the remaining links of the Spurs of old were severed. Cameron's most significant capture was Preston North End's left-back, Sandy Tait. Tait was twenty-six years old when he came south at the start of the 1899-1900 football season and he was destined to play a major part in the Tottenham Hotspur team which finally wrote the club's name into the ranks of the great football sides of the dawn of this century. In addition to Tait, Cameron also signed up a fair-haired Irish international left-winger J. Kirwan, who had played with him at Everton, and an inside-left from Ayrshire, D. Copeland. With Welshman, J. L. Jones, they formed the most

Tottenham Hotspur's manager around the turn of the century was John Cameron, also secretary of the National Union of Association Players, the forerunner of the present Professional Footballers' Association.

talented left-sided attack in English football. In goal, Cameron had the Southampton goalkeeper Clawley who was to figure in a disputed FA Cup Final goal in 1901. With these players, together with himself Cameron built his team. At right-back

was a big Scotsman called Harry Erentz while Tom Morris played at right-half after joining Spurs from Gainsborough. Tom Smith was another man to come from Preston North End. The right-winger would sprint to the by-line before slinging over perfect crosses.

In that 1899-1900 season Tottenham Hotspur played sixty-eight matches and won forty-eight of them, scoring 200 goals into the bargain. Only in the first round of the FA Cup did they do really badly and then it was Proud Preston — the Old Invincibles — who beat them 1-0. As 1899-1900 was the season in which Spurs adopted their present white shirts and navy blue shorts — Preston's colours — it is safe to assume that Tottenham, along with the rest of football, still held the team which won both the League and Cup in 1888-9, in high esteem.

But 1899-1900 was the season when Spurs won their own first major honour. They took the Southern League championship by winning twenty and drawing four of their twenty-eight matches and scoring sixty-seven goals with twenty-six against. Until 1920 — when it was used to form the Third Division South — the Southern League was the premier competition outside the Football League. At the turn of the century only Arsenal, who were then Woolwich Arsenal, of the southern clubs played in the Football League and this opened the door for Tottenham to become the first non-League team to win the FA Cup since the formation of the Football League in 1888. Indeed, the last time a southern club had won the trophy was in the year of Spurs' own formation when Old Etonians won it.

In the summer of 1900, Cameron signed a twenty-two-year-old centre-forward called Alexander Brown who had seen service with Preston and Portsmouth. He came from the same Ayrshire village as Sandy Tait. Brown could do little to help Spurs retain the Southern League title. Before Christmas it became obvious that they would have to work a miracle to get back into the running and in the end they finished fifth — which was higher than they dared have hoped at one stage.

SPURS FIRST FA CUP

If success in the Southern League was to elude the Spurs of 1900-1, then the White Hart Lane club was to give its supporters plenty to cheer about in the FA Cup. Their first round tie with Preston could not be played until 9 February 1901, owing to the death of Queen Victoria. As British history moved into a new era, so did Tottenham Hotspur Football Club. In the first round match at White Hart Lane it took a disputed goal by Alexander Brown to level the scores at 1-1 and earn Spurs a replay with less than ten minutes to play.

In the replay in Lancashire the following Wednesday afternoon, Spurs centre-half and skipper McNaught dropped out through injury and was replaced by Welshman Hughes. So well did Hughes play that McNaught never regained his place while Hughes went on to add to the Welsh caps he had won with Everton. On that bleak February afternoon in Preston almost eighty years ago, Spurs signalled the great things to come. Cameron put them ahead and then Alex Brown, the young centre-forward from the little village of Glenbuck, cracked in a hat-trick and Tottenham were through to the second round with a 4-1 win over the legendary Preston North End club.

In the second round Spurs again faced Lancashire opposition — this time the FA Cup holders, Bury! Bury fielded ten of the side which had beaten Southampton 4-0 at Crystal Palace the previous season and when they took the lead after only two minutes, it looked as though Spurs interest in the FA Cup had come to a swift end. But after thirty minutes Tottenham drew level when Tom Smith made one of his characteristic dashes down the right wing and clipped over a centre for Brown to volley home past Thompson. Twenty thousand White Hart Lane spectators watched enthralled as the two sides hammered away at each other and before an hour had been played Brown was in the right position again and Thompson was again fishing the ball out of the Bury net. It proved the winning goal. Tottenham had done the seemingly impossible and knocked out the FA Cup holders at the first attempt.

Tottenham had to visit Elm Park, Reading for the third round hurdle and were lucky to escape with a 1-1 draw, particularly when the referee gave a goal kick after Tait had used his hand to divert a Reading effort that had 'goal' written all over it. The replay at White Hart Lane proved less difficult for Spurs once Copeland had put them ahead. Brown scored goals two and three and Tottenham marched into the semi-final of the FA Cup for the first time in their history. Indeed, apart from 1898-9 when Stoke beat them 4-1 in the quarter-finals, Spurs had never got beyond the first round proper.

On Easter Monday 1901, Spurs met West Bromwich Albion at Villa Park in front of more than 45,000 spectators. There was no contest — Alex-

ander Brown scored all the goals which gave Spurs a 4-0 win — as West Brom were humiliated with a wonderful display of tight, accurate passing by the Southern League side. Spurs were in the FA Cup Final! They met Sheffield United, the team of nine internationals which had finished just two points behind Aston Villa, the First Division champions in 1900. United had beaten Villa 3-0 in the semi-final after a 2-2 draw in their first meeting. In the Sheffield team was twenty-two stone Billy Foulke in goal, 'Nudger' Needham, the legendary wing-half, and inside-left Fred Priest.

But perhaps the central figure in the match played at the Crystal Palace was Mr Kingscott, the Derby-based referee. It was a decision by him that gave Sheffield United a highly-debatable equaliser after Spurs had taken the lead. It was a decision still remembered today as one of the most controversial of any FA Cup Final. The crowd for the 1901 final was a staggering 114,000 according to the newspapers, although the official attendance has been given as 110,820. Either way it was a world record at the time. The *Daily Graphic* reported: 'From the Midlands, from Yorkshire, from the great towns that form the greater town of London, the army of footballers streamed along the lines of communication which led to Sydenham until 114,000 were gathered around the big green board of turf....' The crowd, the reporter said, 'resembled a waving field of corn.'

◄ *Scenes from the controversial 1901 FA Cup Final at Crystal Palace, when Spurs drew 2-2 with Sheffield United before winning the replay 3-1.*

Spurs victorious 1901 FA Cup winning team. Back row (left to right, players only): Erentz, Clawley, Tait; Middle row: Cameron, Morris, Hughes, Jones, Kirwan; Front Row: Smith, Brown, Copeland. Sandy Brown scored in every round.

▼

After only ten minutes, Priest put Sheffield ahead, 'a daisycutter' reported the *Daily Graphic*. But after twenty-five minutes, the inevitable goal from Brown had levelled the tie at 1-1. Five minutes after half-time, Brown was on target yet again with a thunderous shot which left Foulke completely beaten as it whistled into the Sheffield United net. And that might have been that, had it not been for Mr Kingscott. From the restart, Lipsham went away on the Sheffield United left and tested Clawley with a difficult shot. The Tottenham goalkeeper juggled with the ball and after Sheffield's right-winger Bennett had jostled him, the Spurs goalkeeper finally scrambled the ball away for a corner. Or at least that was what the linesman, perfectly placed, had signalled. But to Spurs' — and United's — amazement, Mr Kingscott was pointing to the centre-spot. The Derby referee had awarded Sheffield an equaliser and refused to confirm it with the linesman who was still signalling a corner.

> *Tottenham Hotspur's 1901 FA Cup-winning side was: Clawley; Erentz, Tait; Morris, Hughes, Jones; Smith, Cameron, Brown, Copeland, Kirwan. The two 'Sandys' – Tait and Brown – came from the same Ayrshire village of Glenbuck.*

The score remained at 2-2 and with controversy still raging, the FA made two surprise decisions. First the replay was staged at Bolton Wanderers ground the following Saturday, where less than 30,000 people could see the game; and Mr Kingscott was chosen to officiate in the replay. On 27 April 1901, on a cold, wet day, Spurs and Sheffield United tried again and again Spurs were a goal down early on when Priest followed up his Crystal Palace effort with another goal. But in the second half, Spurs came into their own and gave the sort of exhibition which had got them to the final in the first place. Cameron, Smith and, of course, Brown, scored to give Tottenham Hotspur a 3-1 victory. Brown had scored in every round and his fifteen goals was still a record in the 1970s. Welshman J. L. Jones stepped up to receive the FA Cup from Lord Kinnaird, the captain of the Old Etonians side which had last brought the Cup south and in the Tottenham High Road at 2am the following morning, the crowds waited to welcome home the victorious Hotspur

> *When the victorious Spurs Cup-winning side arrived home in the early hours of the following morning, ecstatic supporters unharnessed the horses which pulled their transport and took over to haul their heroes the last few hundred yards.*

Spurs bid to retain the FA Cup in 1902 fell at the first hurdle. But they did win the Sheriff of London Shield. Welsh skipper J. L. Jones is the player with his hand on the trophy.

side — probably under the very lamp post where the club had been spawned less than twenty years earlier by those schoolboys who were now grown men. How they must have marvelled at the meteoric rise of their club.

FA Cup winners in 1901 and Southern League champions the year before, it seemed that Spurs' obvious choice was to apply for election to the Football League, then with a First and a Second Division of eighteen clubs each and containing such terms as Glossop North End, Burton United and Gainsborough, as well as more familiar names like Aston Villa, Derby County, Wolves and Sunderland. But Tottenham chose to stay with the Southern League. For the next seven seasons the club stagnated while the Southern League refused admission to Chelsea and Clapton Orient, both teams joining Woolwich Arsenal and Fulham in the Football League.

In 1902 Spurs fell at the first hurdle in an attempt to retain the FA Cup, although in 1903 and 1904 they reached the quarter-final stages. It was the Cup which gave Spurs supporters their only chance of excitement and in February 1904 that excitement went too far and resulted in Spurs being fined £350 and ordered to replay a second round match at their opponents ground. The visitors were mighty Aston Villa who came to White Hart Lane after Spurs had beaten Everton at Goodison Park in the first round. The crowd to see Villa, FA Cup semi-finalists and First Division runners-up the previous season, was enormous and at half-time they spilled onto the pitch. Efforts to clear the ground failed and the game could not restart. Eventually, referee Jack Howcroft had no option but to abandon the match and the Football Association ordered Spurs to take it to Villa Park as well as imposing a hefty fine. Spurs won the replay but after drawing 1-1 with

Sheffield Wednesday (then called simply The Wednesday) at White Hart Lane, they lost the quarter-final replay in Sheffield 2-0.

INTO THE FOOTBALL LEAGUE

All this time, Spurs were becoming increasingly frustrated by what they saw as the Southern League's refusal to move with the times and become a viable opposition to the Football League. Matters came to a head in the close season of 1908 and Tottenham Hotspur withdrew from the Southern League and applied for the Football League itself. One can imagine their horror when the Football League turned down Spurs' application and when the North London club went back to the Southern League, they too, refused to re-admit them. With less than a month to go to the start of the new season, Spurs had a team and a ground as good as any in the country — but no-one to play against.

Tottenham Hotspur supporters to this day, probably do not realise the debt that their club owes to Stoke City. Although Stoke had finished tenth in the Second Division in 1907-8, only they knew what problems they were suffering. Stoke had little support and with the new season looming up, the club resigned from the Second Division, unable to carry on through financial difficulties. Spurs immediately re-applied and along with Bradford Park Avenue (Bradford City had just won promotion to the First Division), they were elected to the Second Division, although they tied three times with bottom club Lincoln City before the Management Committee gave the casting vote to Spurs. Lincoln, original members of the Second Division in 1892, were understandably angry at being booted out.

The Tottenham side to play the club's first-ever Football League match (at home to Wolves on 1 September 1908) was: Hewitson; Coquet, Burton; Morris, Steel (D), Darnell; Walton, V. J. Woodward, Macfarlane, Steel (R), Middlemiss. The ten professionals each received £4.

On Tuesday 1 September 1908, Tottenham Hotspur played their first Football League match at home to Wolverhampton Wanderers. Although finishing ninth in the Second Division in 1907-8, Wolves had won the FA Cup with a sensational 3-1 win over First Division Newcastle United at Crystal

Palace. Of the side which had won the FA Cup in 1901 only right-half Morris remained, although Cameron was still manager. One name in that first Spurs team is still a legend today — the amateur Vivian Woodward. Woodward had gained forty amateur caps for England and sixteen full international caps, and during Spurs first season in the Football League he was capped five more times. He later won two more with Chelsea to bring his total to twenty-three. A powerful scorer, Woodward found the net seventy times in international matches alone and he twice skippered England to victory in the Olympic Games.

Spurs were an instant success in the Second Division. Wherever they went the London club drew big crowds and from the start of the season Tottenham were up with the leaders until in the last week of the 1908-9 season, the two places for promotion rested with Spurs, Bolton Wanderers and West Bromwich Albion. Incredibly, all three clubs had to play Derby County that week and the Rams won one, drew one and lost one. The important thing was that it was Spurs who managed a point in a thrilling 1-1 draw. It was enough to give them First Division football at the first attempt — by just ·02 of a goal! The final Second Division table for that season makes interesting reading:

		P	W	D	L	F	A	Pts
1	Bolton	38	24	4	10	59	28	52
2	Tottenham	38	20	11	7	67	32	51
3	West Brom	38	19	13	6	56	27	51
4	Hull City	38	19	6	13	63	39	44
5	Derby Co	38	16	11	11	55	41	43
6	Oldham A	38	17	6	15	55	43	40
7	Wolves	38	14	11	13	56	48	39
8	Glossop NE	38	15	8	15	57	53	38
9	Gainsborough	38	15	8	15	49	70	38
10	Fulham	38	13	11	14	58	48	37
11	Birmingham	38	14	9	15	58	61	37
12	Leeds City	38	14	7	17	43	53	35
13	Grimsby	38	14	7	17	41	54	35
14	Burnley	38	13	7	18	51	58	33
15	Clapton O	38	12	9	17	37	49	33
16	Bradford PA	38	13	6	19	51	59	32
17	Barnsley	38	11	10	17	48	57	32
18	Stockport	38	14	3	21	39	71	31
19	Chesterfield	38	11	8	19	37	67	30
20	Blackpool	38	9	11	18	46	68	29

Tottenham Hotspur had more than justified the faith which the Football League had placed in them. It is difficult to see how Lincoln City would have strengthened the Second Division in the way that Spurs did. The close season of 1909 saw Spurs embark on a summer tour to Argentina where they

were agreeably surprised at the standard of the local teams. In addition Spurs played two exhibition matches with Everton who were also on tour.

At home there was another happy event when the financial restrictions over the building of a new stand on the western side of the White Hart Lane ground were overcome and when Spurs kicked off their first season in the First Division they did so in front of the biggest grandstand in the country, a stand which provided seating accommodation for 5,000 spectators. The fighting cock emblem of Spurs which now adorns the East Stand at White Hart Lane, first went to roost on top of that West Stand of the early 1900s.

But there had to be something to cloud the early golden years of Spurs and the bombshell was dropped by Vivian Woodward who announced his retirement without having kicked a ball in the First Division. Spurs were stunned at his decision and late in the season they were also bitter when Woodward suddenly decided to resume his career with neighbouring Chelsea. But all that was in the future. Spurs first match in the First Division was at Sunderland where they lost 3-1.

Although Tottenham did not take the First Division by storm — as they had done the Southern League and the Second Division — the season was still a thrilling one. This time, though, it was a fight against a quick return to the Second Division which set the pulses racing. Among their fellow strugglers were Arsenal and Chelsea and it was a game between Spurs and Chelsea at White Hart Lane late in the season which resolved part of the issue. It was also a game which threw up two of those delightful little coincidences of which football is so full. Playing for Chelsea was Vivian Woodward — much to the chagrin of Spurs players, officials and supporters alike. And in the Spurs team was Percy Humphries who had been snapped up by the Tottenham club when Chelsea had dropped him during the season. Spurs won 2-1 to stay safe and send Chelsea crashing into the Second Division — and the winning goal was scored by Percy Humphries! Eventually Spurs avoided relegation by three points to finish in fifteenth place. The bottom places were:

		P	W	D	L	F	A	Pts
15	Tottenham Hotspur	38	11	10	17	53	69	32
16	Bristol City	38	12	8	18	45	60	32
17	Middlesbrough	38	11	9	18	56	73	31
18	Arsenal	38	11	9	18	37	67	31
19	Chelsea	38	11	7	20	47	70	29
20	Bolton Wanderers	38	9	6	23	44	71	24

The Spurs side which narrowly missed relegation to the Second Division in 1913-14. Several of the players who were to figure in Spurs revival were already at White Hart Lane. Jimmy Cantrell has the ball at his feet and Arthur Grimsdell is fifth from left on the back row.

Spurs found it hard to consolidate their position in the First Division. In 1910-11 they finished fifteenth again; in 1911-12 they climbed to twelfth; but in 1912-13 they slumped to seventeenth position, although they were seven points clear of relegated Notts County who finished next-to-bottom and in 1913-14, Spurs were again in seventeenth position, this time missing the drop by four points.

At the end of that season Spurs went on a tour of Germany — even four months before its outbreak, people did not really think that there would be a war — and when they returned home the Tottenham management set about building a side that would go up the First Division instead of down it. The embryo was there but when an assassin's bullet rang out in Sarajevo to start World War I, it also put paid to Spurs' hopes of early glories. The British

There is a story which says that when Spurs came back from their 1914 close season tour of Germany, they brought back with them a German centre-forward. Before he had time to kick a ball for the club, he was recalled to the German army.

Government decided that the 1914-15 football season could go ahead as a morale-booster for the people, but Tottenham's morale was dented when several of the club's key players volunteered on the tide of patriotic fervour which was sweeping the country. When the season ended, Spurs had lost £4,000 and even worse, they were stuck at the foot of the First Division with Chelsea who had bounced back up from the Second in 1911-12. Spurs had won only eight of their thirty-eight games and had conceded ninety goals.

Alas, Tottenham had to spend four seasons as a Second Division club before they kicked a ball. Although the Scottish League continued throughout the war, the Football League closed down and White Hart Lane became a gas mask factory. But with the war won in 1918 and football set to resume for the 1919-20 season, there was war of a different kind in North London. In 1913 the Football League had permitted Arsenal to move from Plumstead to Highbury and Spurs were annoyed that their old rivals were now in a position to vie for the support of the area's football fans. But to add insult to injury, the League Management Committee then achieved another piece of cuckoo-land legislation just before peacetime football restarted.

They decided that the First and Second Divisions would each be increased by two clubs. The question was whether Barnsley and Wolves (third and fourth in Division Two in 1914-15) would make up the numbers, or whether the last two clubs in Division

One (Chelsea and Spurs) would retain their places. The Football League managed to think up a splendid, if illogical, answer. Chelsea would not be relegated but Spurs would go down. And neither Barnsley nor Wolves would be promoted, but Arsenal, who had finished sixth in Division Two! Coupled with the fact that Spurs had spent £40,000 on ground improvements only to see Arsenal move in just three miles away on land at St John's Divinity College, Highbury, the White Hart Lane club could have been forgiven for thinking that someone somewhere had a grudge against them. Happily, the Tottenham Board of Directors decided that the best thing to do was to get on with putting their club back into the top flight and this they proceeded to do with a vengeance.

With war clouds gathering, Spurs had already been acquiring many of the players who would take them to the top when peace came. In 1913 Bert Bliss and Arthur Grimsdell had signed, Bliss a prolific scorer and Grimsdell a workmanlike wing-half and the engine-room of any team. In 1914 'Fanny' Walden and Jimmy Cantrell signed and were joined by Tommy Banks and Tommy Clay. After the war manager Peter McWilliam, a famous Scottish international wing-half with Newcastle United, added Jimmy Seed and left-winger Jimmy Dimmock, and the great Tottenham Hotspur team of the immediate post war years was together.

> A full Spurs 'team' died in the fighting of World War I. The eleven were: J. Fleming, J. Heddon, A. Hobday, J. Jarvie, E. Lightfoot, W. Lloyd, A. McGregor, W. Tull, F. Weir, A. Wilson, N. Wood.

BETWEEN THE WARS

On Saturday 30 August 1919 Tottenham Hotspur opened their first post-war season with a Second Division match at Coventry City where they won 5-0; on the following Monday evening Leicester City visited White Hart Lane for the first League match there for over four years. Spurs won 4-0 and that was how they went for the rest of the season. Unbeaten at home they dropped just two points at White Hart Lane by drawing with Blackpool and Birmingham City and scoring sixty goals with just eleven against. At the end of the season Tottenham were Second Division champions with seventy

Tottenham's 1919-20 side which returned to the First Division in the first post-war season: Back row (left to right): Archibald, Smith, Jacques, Grimsdell, Lowe, Brown. Front row: McDonald, Banks, Seed, Cantrell, Bliss, Chipperfield.

points — six clear of runner-up Huddersfield Town — and in all they had scored 102 League goals. In the FA Cup Spurs had reached the quarter-finals before losing by the only goal of a hard-fought match against Aston Villa at White Hart Lane. To add to their disappointment, that lone goal had been scored by Tommy Clay who sliced the ball into his own net leaving Jacques helpless to prevent an untidy Villa victory.

> *Spurs team for the first Football League match after the end of World War I (away to Coventry City on 30 August 1919) was: Jacques; Clay, Pearson; Smith, Minter, Grimsdell; Walden, Lindsay, Cantrell, Bliss and Chipperfield.*

Back in the First Division after five years — but only one playing season — Spurs this time did not flounder in the highest company, although Blackburn Rovers won the first First Division match of the 1920-1 season at White Hart Lane by the narrowest of margins. Although Tottenham finished in sixth position, their highest in the First Division, it was obvious that by the New Year their only real hopes of success lay in the FA Cup. In the first round Spurs hammered a luckless Bristol Rovers side 6-2. Rovers lost a player early on through injury and in the days before substitutes were thought of, the West Country club had to battle on with ten men.

It may seem strange in the 1980s to recall that Bradford City were once a First Division side and that they won the FA Cup in 1911. At any rate, the Yorkshire club provided Tottenham Hotspur with stiff opposition in the second round of the 1920-1 competition. At White Hart Lane Spurs scored four goals to win the tie but the gritty Yorkshiremen made them fight every inch of the way. It was the sheer brilliance of Jimmy Seed which won the day with a magnificent performance crowned by a superb hat-trick. Tommy Banks hit the fourth goal for Spurs and they went through to meet Southend

United in the third round. Southend, like Spurs, had been members of the Southern League and they entertained Tottenham as members of the newly-formed Third Division.

At the Kursaal, Southend held on for sixty minutes, during which time they were awarded a penalty which they missed after the referee himself placed the ball on the penalty spot and refused to allow the Southend forward who stepped up to take the kick, to adjust it. After that let-off, Spurs went on to win 4-1 with goals from Cantrell, Banks, Bliss and Seed, although the final margin flattered a somewhat subdued Tottenham side.

The team which won the FA Cup for Tottenham Hotspur in 1921 was: Hunter; Clay, McDonald; Smith, Walters, Grimsdell; Banks, Seed, Cantrell, Bliss, Dimmock. The club presented each member of the team with a gold watch. There was special mention for the team's trainer Billy Minter who had scored 99 goals as a player from 1908 to 1920.

The quarter-final brought a repeat of the previous season's match with Aston Villa at White Hart Lane. Over 51,000 fans paid nearly £7,000 to see Spurs reverse the 1-0 scoreline in their favour. Tommy Banks scored the vital goal and in the Spurs goal, Hunter, standing in for the injured Jacques played so well that he retained his place and went on to win an FA Cup winners' medal.

Tottenham Hotspur reached their second FA Cup semi-final where they met Preston North End at Hillsborough, Sheffield. In the other semi-final Wolverhampton Wanderers and Cardiff City played each other at Old Trafford after failing to score a goal in their first encounter, Wolves eventually winning 3-1. But Spurs needed no second chance. Two blistering goals by Bert Bliss sealed Preston's fate and the 2-1 scoreline did not reflect the dominance which Spurs had on the game.

The 1921 FA Cup Final was played at Chelsea's Stamford Bridge ground on 23 April before over 72,000 spectators who paid almost £13,500 to see little Jimmy Dimmock score the only goal of the game. Dimmock was born in the shadow of Spurs' ground and in this, only his second season, he achieved something usually reserved for the heroes of the more imaginative boys' comics.

The game was spoiled by incessant rain and the fact that Wolves were just an average Second Division team at the time. After King George V and the future King George VI met the teams, the rain continued to bucket down and for the whole of the first half both teams found conditions difficult. Remember this was not Wembley's green sward, especially reserved for the occasion, but a ground on which football had been played every Saturday for nearly nine months. After fifty-two minutes Bliss hit the ball out to Dimmock on the Spurs left and the winger cut past the Wolves defence, drove inside, and then released a shot from about fifteen yards and then watched as the ball slewed along the greasy surface and flew past George and into the Wolves net. Forty minutes later Arthur Grimsdell was receiving the FA Cup from the hands of the King.

Jimmy Dimmock, born in the shadow of Spurs ground, who scored the winning goal for Tottenham in the 1921 FA Cup Final in only his second season at White Hart Lane.

Twenty years earlier, the Tottenham High Road had witnessed scenes of jubilation as Tottenham brought the FA Cup home. Now those scenes were repeated with the FA Cup bearing the same blue and white ribbons which had adorned the previous trophy. Of that 1901 team, all but the now-deceased goalkeeper George Clawley were invited to a celebration at the Holborn Restaurant. The world had changed a great deal since the first Hotspur FC team had taken the field in 1882. But the traditions of courage, skill and vision epitomised by Harry Hotspur, lived on.

From Second Division champions in 1920 to FA Cup winners in 1921, Tottenham Hotspur aimed for the ultimate pinnacle of the First Division championship when the 1921-2 season opened. They failed by just six points, although they went near to retaining the FA Cup for another year. By losing three of the four points available in their two League matches with Liverpool, Tottenham left only the FA Cup open to them as a means of maintaining the glorious progress they had enjoyed since 1919. At first, it looked as though Spurs might go the whole distance in the Cup. Brentford, Watford and Manchester City were each systematically removed in the first three rounds until Spurs drew Cardiff City at Ninian Park in the fourth round. Jimmy Seed went to Wales to put Spurs ahead but in the dying stages of the match Cardiff equalised to force a replay. With 55,000 crammed inside, White Hart Lane was bursting at the seams in the return match.

Cardiff were a respectable First Division side who would finish fourth that season and it seemed that all London wanted to see the visitors from the Principality. The game was hard but fair and with a few minutes left, Tottenham's Wilson hit home the winner to give them a 2-1 victory and put them into their third FA Cup semi-final against Preston North End at Sheffield Wednesday's Hillsborough stadium.

Just as they had suffered a disputed referee's decision in the 1901 FA Cup Final, so Tottenham were again apparently wronged in the 1922 semi-final. With the score at 1-1 in the second half, Bliss crashed the ball home, only to see the referee put the whistle to his lips to disallow the 'goal'. The referee said that he had already halted play before Bliss shot, so that an injured Preston player could be treated. But Spurs players were adamant that the whistle went *after* Bliss had connected with the ball. Thus spurred, Preston went away to score the winner and Tottenham had nothing to show for the season. It was a decision, however well-intentioned, that quickened the decline of the magnificent Tottenham Hotspur team which had lost four years to World War I. Had football been resumed in 1915-16 when McWilliam had the nucleus of his

side together, there is no telling what glories might have covered White Hart Lane. Those lost years meant that the Spurs ran out of steam long before they had achieved all that was rightly theirs.

> *Spurs almost became the victims of a sensational giantkilling act in 1923 when nearly 24,000 White Hart Lane spectators saw Midland League Worksop Town all but knock Spurs out of the FA Cup. With no goals scored and just four minutes left, Worksop's Rippon chipped the ball over goalkeeper Blake's head, only to see it hit the crossbar and bounce clear. In the replay, also at White Hart Lane, Spurs made no mistake with a 9-0 win but Worksop's £1,050 share of the two 'gates' wiped out the tiny club's debts for that season.*

For the next five seasons Tottenham Hotspur finished no higher than twelfth and as low as fifteenth on two occasions. In 1923 they reached the quarter-final of the FA Cup but lost 1-0 to Derby County at White Hart Lane. The middle and late twenties were lean years for Spurs and in 1928 they found themselves twenty-first in the First Division with just one point more than bottom club Middlesbrough. Strangely, Peter McWilliam had left Spurs for Middlesbrough in 1927 when the North-Easterners had offered to double the salary which Spurs paid their manager. Spurs trainer Billy Minter was promoted to take his place and one of his first jobs was to transfer Seed — who had won England caps — to Sheffield Wednesday. Seed had been unable to regain his place after injury and Tottenham did a foolish thing in letting him go. He went on to play well and could have served White Hart Lane well over the coming difficult years.

Spurs loss of First Division status in 1928 was little short of sensational. They had reached the quarter-final of the FA Cup and had just thrashed the eventual champions Everton 5-2 at Goodison Park. By Easter they stood seventh in the First Division, higher than they had been for years. At the end of the season they were relegated, admittedly with more points than any other relegated club in the history of the Football League. So what went wrong? The turning point had come on 3 March 1928 when Spurs faced the redoubtable Huddersfield Town team in the FA Cup quarter-final and lost 6-1. Even allowing for the fact that Huddersfield were champions in 1924-5-6 and runners-up in 1927 and 1928, it takes some explaining how a First Division side could lose by that margin in the last eight of the FA Cup. Spurs historians blame the 'special training' in the snow-covered peaks of Buxton in Derbyshire as the cause. Weakened by this, Tottenham crashed and never recovered from the shock of such a humiliating defeat. Three points from their last seven matches ensured that they finished just below Portsmouth in one of the tightest-ever scrambles at the foot of the First Division. Two more points would have taken them up to a respectable fourteenth place. In contrast, Jimmy Seed's Sheffield Wednesday had won seventeen points from their last ten games to go from a seemingly hopeless position at the foot of the table to fourteenth spot.

There was no instant return for Tottenham Hotspur this time. The side had spent only two previous seasons in the Second Division, winning promotion each time. At the end of the 1920s and the beginning of the 1930s. Spurs shared in the world depression. In 1928-9 and 1929-30 Spurs finished tenth and twelfth respectively before missing promotion by just three points in 1930-1. In 1931-2 they finished eighth and it was not until 1932-3 — their fifth consecutive season in the Second Division — that they finally won their way back to the First by finishing runners-up to Stoke

Willie Evans who scored 28 goals – including ten penalties – as Spurs won promotion in 1932-3.

Spurs forward line of 1933-4 when the club finished third in the First Division. (left to right): Evans, Hall, Hunt, McCormick, O'Callaghan. Willie Hall cost Spurs £500 when he was capped against France that season. Tottenham had to pay that amount to his former club, Notts County.

Spurs half-back line of 1933-4 (left to right): Evans, Rowe, Meads. Like Willie Hall, Arthur Rowe was also capped for England against France in December of that season.

The last line of defence. Goalkeeper Nicholls and full-backs Felton (left) and Whatley, who completed a successful Tottenham line-up in 1933-4.

Percy Smith, the former Bury manager, who guided Spurs back into the First Division in 1932-3. He resigned in 1935 after Spurs dropped back to the Second Division.

City, the side which had made way for them in 1908.

Spurs new manager during their sojourn in the Second Division was Percy Smith who had joined the club from Bury to take over from Billy Minter who was glad to have rid of the job. Minter became assistant secretary and Smith set about re-shaping the team of veteran players which he had inherited. All great teams reach a stage where they have to be dismantled and rebuilt — witness the Spurs side which won the 'double' — and Smith knew that he had to look long and hard at the Tottenham team.

> *Percy Smith's first-choice Spurs eleven when they finished third in Division Two in 1930-1 was: Spiers; Lyons, Hodgkinson; Meads, Messer, Skitt; Davies, O'Callaghan, Harper, Cook, Bellamy. Spurs missed promotion by only three points.*

The blend was altered, particularly in defence, and at the start of 1932-3, Percy Smith knew he had a team which could win its way back to the First Division. Perhaps the most famous of all that new team's names is Arthur Rowe, a tenacious wing-half who would, himself, be associated as a manager with the famous 'push and run' Spurs team after World War II. Rowe was a local boy who joined Tottenham as a junior and soon earned his first full England cap. He was one of the best wing halves of the 1930s. George Hunt and Willie Evans led the way back to Division One with goals galore.

Of the final Tottenham League tally of ninety-six, Hunt bagged thirty-six and Evans twenty-eight, including ten penalties. If Spurs had not lost their first four away matches they would certainly have been Second Division champions in 1933. But the important thing was that White Hart Lane would once again ring to the cheers of First Division crowds.

Once safely back in the First Division, Tottenham soon began to establish themselves and by the New Year of 1934 they stood in third place, three points behind Arsenal who headed the table. In December 1933, Arthur Rowe and Willie Hall played for England against France and although Spurs had to pay Hall's former club Notts County £500 as part of a transfer deal agreement if the player was capped, it looked like a happy 1934 for the Tottenham club.

But the ultimate happiness of a First Division title was not to be. In the New Year, Arsenal took control and won the League three points clear of Huddersfield and ten ahead of Spurs who finished in third place. In the FA Cup, Spurs had gone out in the fifth round to Aston Villa. Nevertheless, it was a bright beginning for a newly-promoted club, and Tottenham looked forward to 1934-5 with obvious relish. Incredibly, Spurs finished bottom of the First Division. After just one season of near-glory the White Hart Lane club rocketed to the foot of the table. They waited until their fifth match for their first win; lost Arthur Rowe through injury for much of the season; used a total of thirty-six players in the first team — always the hallmark of a struggling club — and finished rock bottom three points behind Leicester City who went down with them and with a goals against total of ninety-three. But perhaps the cruellest rub for the club's faithful supporters was when Arsenal made the short trip across North London and trounced Spurs 6-0 in front of a shame-faced White Hart Lane crowd. In the 1935 close season Percy Smith resigned after taking Spurs to glory and then seeing them drop to the depths.

The man who replaced him as Tottenham Hotspur manager for the start of 1935-6 was Jack Tresadern, the man who had played left-half for West Ham United in the famous 1923 'White Horse' FA Cup Final — the first at Wembley Stadium. A former England international, Tresadern had managed Northampton Town and Crystal Palace and was no stranger to the tough, insecure world of running a professional soccer team. But Tresadern's only real claim to note in the long history of Tottenham Hotspur Football Club was that he dropped leading scorer and darling of the White Hart Lane fans, George Hunt. It was an unpopular move and when it became obvious that he was not the man to get Tottenham back into the

The Spurs team which finished fifth in the Second Division in 1935-6. Back row (left to right): Howe, Channell, Taylor, Hunt, Whatley, Phypers. Front row: Sargent, A. Hall, Morrison, W. Hall, Evans, Rowe. Spurs darling George Hunt (in suit) was sensationally dropped by new manager Jack Tresadern.

First Division, he was replaced in 1938 by Peter McWilliam, the man who had guided them to the FA Cup in 1921.

It is one of football's little ironies that while Spurs were being relegated to the Second Division, a spanking new double-decker stand was springing up on the east side of White Hart Lane. The problem concerning this prestigious new piece of architecture was that Spurs had gone into debt to the tune of £60,000 to pay for it. It was fortunate that Spurs could still command good crowds even after they had been relegated.

There were some brighter moments. Spurs reached the quarter-finals of the FA Cup in 1936, 1937 and 1938 and in 1938 the Cup holders Sunderland drew a crowd of 75,038 to White Hart Lane before winning with the only goal of the game. In the Second Division, Spurs rose to fifth place in

> *Spurs caused a sensation in 1937 when they beat First Division Portsmouth 5-0 at Fratton Park in the third round of the FA Cup. The team which caused the upset was: Hall; Ward, Whatley; Buckingham, Rowe, Grice; McCormick, Meek, Morrison, Duncan, Miller. Morrison scored a hat-trick and Buckingham went on to become a manager with Fulham, West Brom and Ajax Amsterdam where he 'discovered' Johan Cruyff.*

1936 and 1938, and in November 1938, Willie Hall played in another match for England. The first one had been at White Hart Lane against France in 1933 when England won 4-1. This time Hall was to write his name into the record books with five successive goals against Ireland at Old Trafford, including a hat-trick in less than four minutes. Sadly, Hall had not long to live. An illness led to his death in the early years of World War II.

It was the war which now stood in Peter McWilliam's way, just as it had done in 1914. In 1938-9 he steered Tottenham to eighth place in the Second Division, seven points behind promoted

Spurs Reserves 1937-8. Back row (left to right): Ludford, Dann, Spellman, Hooper, Martin, Reeves, Jeffrey. Front row: McCormick, Meek, Hunt, A. Hall, Wilkins, Hitchens.

Spurs of 1938-9. Vic Buckingham, the man who later discovered the legendary Dutchman, Johan Cruyff, is second from the right on the back row. Willie Hall (with ball) scored a record five successive goals for England against Ireland in November that season, including a hat-trick in less than four minutes.

club Sheffield United. At the same time he was assembling the players who would carry Tottenham's hopes in the years following the war. From his nursery at Northfleet came Ted Ditchburn, Les Bennett, Ronnie Burgess, Bill Nicholson, Les Medley — all component parts of the Arthur Rowe side of the early 1950s.

The 1939-40 football season lasted just two Saturdays before German Panzers went into action against Polish cavalry and the Football League shut up shop for the next seven seasons. White Hart Lane became a home for Arsenal when Highbury was made into an ARP centre, and the last traces of the bitterness between the two clubs which went back to 1919 were forgotten. Arsenal, Spurs, indeed the whole free world, had more important enemies to beat.

RETURN TO THE TOP

Football during World War II was a motley affair. Players appeared for clubs near where they were stationed and some quite insignificant teams had the rare distinction of fielding international players. When wartime competitions got underway they bore little resemblance to the peacetime Football League, being chopped up into much smaller regional divisions.

The football played between 1939 and 1945 was of doubtful parentage but, for what it is worth, Spurs name cropped up a few times in the honours table. In 1939-40 Tottenham Hotspur won the South 'C' Section of the Football League; in 1943-4 they won the Southern Section; and in 1944-5 they

took the Southern Section title again. There were quite a few other honours which came to White Hart Lane during those war years — but they were won by Arsenal who, of course, were sharing Tottenham's home for the duration.

In the first season of peace in 1945-6, the Football League was still full of such quaint divisions as Third Division South (Northern Section) and the proper four-division league did not resume until 1946-7. But the FA Cup *did* restart in 1945-6 and it was the only season when the competition has been fought out on a two-legged basis up to and including the quarter-final. Tottenham went out at the first hurdle. After 2-2 with Brentford at White Hart Lane, Spurs lost the second-leg 2-0 at Griffin Park, while Brentford went right through to the sixth round before being beaten 9-4 on aggregate by Charlton Athletic, the eventual losing finalists of the first post-war FA Cup Final.

In the following season's FA Cup, Tottenham fared no better. Although the competition was now back to its familiar 'instant death' approach, Spurs still had to play two matches in the third round against Stoke City. At White Hart Lane, Spurs managed a 2-2 draw against a Stoke side which would finish fourth in Division One that season. At the Victoria Ground, Stanley Matthews scored one of his rare goals to send Spurs out 1-0.

In the Second Division Tottenham Hotspur did reasonably well in 1946-7, finishing sixth — fourteen points behind the champions Manchester City

— with a final league record of P42 W17 D14 L11 F65 A53 Pts 48. Already the famous Spurs 'push and run' team was taking shape with Ditchburn, Nicholson, Burgess, Bennett and Medley together with left-back Ron Willis. In 1947-8, Spurs finished eighth, this time fifteen points adrift of Second Division champions Birmingham City, although just another four points would have taken the Tottenham side up into fifth place.

In the 1947-8 FA Cup, Tottenham Hotspur made rapid progress to reach the semi-finals again. In the third round Spurs were drawn against Bolton Wanderers at Burnden Park — scene of Tottenham's eventual FA Cup win in the 1901 replay against Sheffield United. Spurs won 2-0 and earned the right to meet West Bromwich Albion in the next stage of the competition. Another fine performance saw Spurs through 3-1 at White Hart Lane, and then Leicester City came to North London for the fifth round and were beaten 5-2. In these first three cup-ties, Les Duquemin, a centre-forward from the Channel Islands, scored seven times. At the Dell, in the sixth round, Len Bennett scored the only goal of the game to knock out Southampton and put Spurs in the last four.

The semi-final hurdle was Blackpool at Villa Park. Blackpool were a First Division side of some distinction with players like Harry Johnston, Stanley Mortenson, Eddie Shimwell and Stanley Matthews. Tottenham's response to this daunting First Division challenge was to take the lead through Duquemin, a lead which they held until there was less than five minutes remaining on the referee's watch. Then Stan Mortenson won a tussle with Vic Buckingham and hit a shot towards the Tottenham goal. Ditchburn had come out of his goal and the ball squeezed past him for a fortunate equaliser from Blackpool's point of view. It was a terrible moment to concede a goal and it gave Blackpool new life. In extra-time Blackpool played more like everyone knew they could and twice Mortenson beat Ditchburn to make the final score 3-1.

Besides knocking Spurs out of the FA Cup, that defeat probably also cost them a First Division place. Before the Villa Park game Tottenham had taken thirty-five points from thirty games. After the defeat they won only nine points from their remaining twelve League matches to slump down the table. But the talent was there. The ability to take the Second Division by storm was apparent, if only Tottenham could maintain some consistency.

In 1948-9 Spurs began to climb. Under the captaincy of Ron Burgess — the Welsh international had blossomed into one of the greatest Spurs players of all time — and the management of former Arsenal player Joe Hulme, Tottenham finished fifth in the Second Division. Although they were seven points behind champions Fulham, Totten-

Spurs 1947-8 team which finished eighth in the Second Division. Back row (left to right): Ludford, Nicholson, Willis, Ditchburn, Buckingham, Burgess, Cecil Poynton (trainer). Front row: Jones, Dix, Rundle, Joe Hulme (manager), Bennett, Stevens, Chisholm. Jack Chisholm later went to Plymouth and found fame as one of the first bearded professional footballers.

ham had closed the gap on the leaders considerably in comparison with previous years.

Ted Ditchburn was by now one of the best goalkeepers in the Football League and Spurs had gone into their old home of the Southern League to capture centre-half Harry Clarke from Lovells Athletic. Len Duquemin was becoming a goalscorer to rank with any in the League and the scheming of Les Bennett and Eddie Baily saw that he had the best possible service. On the wings, Les Medley and Sonny Walters, who had returned to the club from National Service, completed a fearsome Tottenham forward line, although it was still a forward line which had less teeth away from White Hart Lane. Spurs had won only three away matches in their 1948-9 Football League campaign and they knew that a rapid improvement on opponent's grounds would have to come before promotion was a serious possibility. In the FA Cup, Spurs lost 3-0 to Arsenal at Highbury in the third round — a bitter pill for many of the club's supporters to swallow.

Just before the end of 1948-9 Spurs had a change of manager when Joe Hulme was unable to continue through illness. He was replaced in the Tottenham hot seat by Arthur Rowe, Spurs centre-half and skipper of pre-war days. Rowe had been coaching in Hungary and had seen at first-hand the development of the game there — a development which all of England would feel to its cost when the Hungarians put thirteen goals past the England team in two matches just over one year apart. Rowe had returned to England and was secretary-manager of Chelmsford when he answered the call from his old club.

The final touch to the Tottenham side which would win promotion in 1949-50 was the signing of Southampton's cultured right-back Alf Ramsey, the man who would later lead England to the 1966 World Cup triumph.

Rowe's approach to the game is summed up in a telegram he sent FA Amateur Cup-finalists Pegasus on the day they first won that trophy — *'Make it simple, make it quick!'*. Rowe's doctrine was all about possession of the ball, doing the simple thing, and doing it quickly. Rowe did away with all sorts of pre-conceptions about how the game should be played in England. He re-wrote the coaching manual with a side whose success was based on sweet, accurate passing. 'If we've got the ball,' Rowe would say, 'then the other side cannot possibly score.'

Every great team has a powerhouse, an engine-room around which everything else revolves, and in the Tottenham Hotspur side of that era, the power-house and engine-room was Ron Burgess. The whole play stemmed from him — the action seemed to bounce off him. Burgess made it simple, made it quick. The hallmark of Rowe's success was that he

achieved it with players who were already on Tottenham's books when he arrived. Apart from Ramsey, the rest of the side had hardly cost a penny.

> **When Spurs won the Second Division title in 1949-50, right-back Alf Ramsey won four England caps against Italy, Scotland, Portugal and Belgium. That summer Eddie Baily also played for England in a World Cup match against Spain.**

By the New Year of 1950 Spurs were ten points ahead of any other team. They had gone over twenty matches without defeat. After opening the season with 4-1 wins over Brentford and Plymouth, Spurs had lost 3-2 to Blackburn. This defeat probably did them good for they put their feet firmly on the ground and never looked back.

Not until, that is, they had all but won promotion. Although Spurs finally took the 1949-50 Second Division title nine points ahead of their nearest rivals Sheffield Wednesday, they lost four of their last five games and with them the chance to establish a new Second Division points record. But instead of bettering their own seventy points of 1920, Tottenham had to be satisfied with sixty-one. The final positions at the top of the 1949-50 Second Division read as follows:

		P	W	D	L	F	A	Pts
1	Tottenham Hotspur	42	27	7	8	81	35	61
3	Sheffield Wednesday	42	18	16	8	67	48	52
3	Sheffield United	42	19	14	9	68	49	52
4	Southampton	42	19	14	9	64	48	52
5	Leeds United	42	17	13	12	54	45	47
6	Preston North End	42	18	9	15	60	49	45

In the FA Cup Tottenham signalled their intentions of taking the following season's First Division by storm when they went through to the fifth round with an epic 5-1 win over First Division Sunderland. Only a hotly-disputed Everton penalty in the sixth round stood between Tottenham Hotspur and another semi-final appearance. But the club was back in the top flight. Nearly seventy years had elapsed since the schoolboys of North London had formed Hotspur FC. Two world wars, five monarchs and a host of changes that made the world almost unrecognisable had run parallel with the emergence of one of the most famous football clubs in the world.

1950-1

When newly-promoted Tottenham Hotspur were soundly beaten 4-1 at home by Blackpool on the opening day of the 1950-1 First Division season, there were plenty of people in the game who were only too delighted to nod their heads knowingly and whisper gently, but firmly, 'I told you so!'. And when, at the end of September, Tottenham were in thirteenth place in the First Division, it looked as though the critics of Arthur Rowe's 'push and run style' — the football which had taken the Second Division by storm the previous season — might well have a point when they declared that Tottenham Hotspur were not faring nearly as well in English football's top flight.

But on that last day of September 1950, Tottenham began a run of eight consecutive victories. They beat Aston Villa 3-2 to begin a sequence which took them to within striking distance of the leading clubs in the First Division. 'Push and run' had at last been proved at the very highest level of club football. Spurs scored eighteen goals in just three matches and their 7-0 win over Newcastle United at White Hart Lane, ranks as one of the greatest-ever performances by any side in a Football League match. Newcastle were to go on to win the FA Cup

that season and the side humiliated by Spurs was the one which went on to triumph at Wembley. Spurs skipper Ronnie Burgess missed that epic game with a leg injury. But he watched from the stand and for the first time began to realise the full potential of Rowe's plan. He said afterwards: 'It was the finest example of football that I have ever seen. I sat absolutely enthralled and I realised for the first time why we had won so many matches with our "push and run" style.'

> In Tottenham's first season back in the First Division in 1950-1, the average attendance at White Hart Lane was an incredible 55,486 – an increase of one thousand per match on the previous year. In the days before floodlighting allowed late kick-offs, particularly in midweek, these figures show the staggering popularity of the Tottenham side of that 'push and run' era.

By the time Christmas 1950 came around, Tottenham were poised to take over the leadership of the First Division and they did so, winning seven points from their four holiday games. Having reached the top of the First Division mountain,

Spurs full-back Willis plays the ball back to his goal-keeper during the 1-0 win over Arsenal at White Hart Lane in December 1950.

over that golden period include: Ditchburn (84), Clarke (84), Ramsey (79), Baily (78), Nicholson (78), Medley (75), Walters (75), Burgess (74), Duquemin (71) and Les Bennett, who suffered a string of niggling injuries, (60). Peter Murphy came from Coventry to play in twenty-five games as an admirable substitute; and when full-back Withers (45 appearances) was injured, Willis stepped into his boots to make forty-one impeccable appearances in the Tottenham rearguard.

In the Tottenham Hotspur side which won the 1950-1 championship, English football saw the tremendous possibilities of 'push and run'. Rowe's period as a coach in Hungary was partly responsible for the adoption of a style which brought success after success to White Hart Lane. Within three years, the brilliant Hungarians would trounce England at Wembley with a similar approach. But still the rest of English Football League clubs stuck to their tried-and-tested styles. The success of Tottenham Hotspur, while acknowledged, was largely ignored. It would prove to be to the cost of English football.

Spurs were in no hurry to leave the peak which they had scaled and there they stayed for the rest of the season

Apart from Blackpool, only Huddersfield Town won at White Hart Lane in 1950-1. And curiously, it was the Yorkshire club which beat Tottenham three times, twice in the League and once in the third round of the FA Cup when Spurs journeyed to Leeds Road in January and lost 2-0. Although a bitter disappointment, that FA Cup defeat was by no means a disaster. In fact, it meant that Tottenham Hotspur could concentrate solely on becoming the First Division champions. Concentrate they did. Despite that shaky start to the season, Spurs lost only seven Football League games in 1950-1. They brought the First Division title to White Hart Lane for the first time in the club's history, winning it with sixty points — the highest total since Spurs arch-rivals Arsenal took the Championship with sixty-six points back in 1930-1. Spurs finished four points clear of their nearest rivals, Manchester United, and they scored eighty-two goals and conceded forty-four. In two seasons, Tottenham had netted 163 League goals as they stormed to two successive championships.

They achieved all this with virtually an unchanged side. The figures for Tottenham appearances out of a possible eighty-four league games

◀ *Tottenham Hotspur 1950-1. The side remained virtually unchanged as Spurs stormed to their second successive championship. Alf Ramsey, later to manage England and be knighted, is the first player on the left of the back row.*

First Division results 1950-1

	H	A
Arsenal	1-0	2-2
Aston Villa	3-2	3-2
Blackpool	1-4	1-0
Bolton	4-2	4-1
Burnley	1-0	0-2
Charlton	1-0	1-1
Chelsea	2-1	2-0
Derby	2-1	1-1
Everton	3-0	2-1
Fulham	2-1	1-0
Huddersfield	0-2	2-3
Liverpool	3-1	1-2
Man Utd	1-0	1-2
Middlesbrough	3-3	1-1
Newcastle	7-0	1-0
Portsmouth	5-1	1-1
Sheffield Wed	1-0	1-1
Stoke	6-1	0-0
Sunderland	1-1	0-0
West Brom	5-0	2-1
Wolves	2-1	1-2

Final League Record

P	W	D	L	F	A	Pts	Pos
42	25	10	7	82	44	60	1st

FA Cup

Rnd 3	Huddersfield Town	(a)	0-2

1951-2

Having won the Second Division title and then the First Division championship in consecutive seasons, Tottenham Hotspur could be reasonably sure that 1951-2 was going to be yet another good year with more trophies to adorn the Boardroom at White Hart Lane. Yet things went wrong and even a late burst of match-winning football late in the season failed to bring a hat-trick of successes to North London, although another couple of wins and a draw would have ensured that the First Division trophy remained with Tottenham for another year.

Tottenham never really recovered from a mid-season reverse when Billy Liddell scored a hat-trick for Liverpool at White Hart Lane and the Anfield club went away with a 3-2 win to shock Spurs into the fact that the League Championship was not there for the taking after all. In their next twelve matches, Tottenham gained only nine points. It was a sequence from which no club could properly expect to recover to the extent of regaining the lead of the First Division.

Newcastle United — the team which had been cruelly destroyed 7-0 at White Hart Lane less than twelve months previously — gained ample revenge. In the First Division match at St James' Park, Newcastle ran rampage and Tottenham caught the train back south still smarting from the sobering lesson of a 7-2 defeat. And in the FA Cup, it was Newcastle who ended Spurs hopes of an extended run. In the third round Spurs had won an easy tie with Third Division (North) side Scunthorpe United. Scunthorpe had only just been admitted to the Football League and went down 3-0 at the Old Show Ground. One round later, Spurs themselves were beaten 3-0 at home to Newcastle.

Yet Tottenham Hotspur played their last twelve matches as though they had an almost divine right to the First Division title. With eight victories, four draws and no defeats, Spurs took twenty points from their last dozen games to pip Arsenal for runners-up position.

It was strange that the turning point for Tottenham's revived fortunes in 1951-2 should begin with a home match against Huddersfield Town — the team which had beaten them three times the previous season and the team which the Tottenham players regarded as something of a 'bogey' side. The game between the two sides at White Hart Lane might have been an uninspiring goalless draw but for a unique incident which put the match into football's folklore of odd facts. Eddie Baily took a corner and drove it hard into the penalty area where

First Division results 1951-2

	H	A
Arsenal	1-2	1-1
Aston Villa	2-0	3-0
Blackpool	2-0	0-1
Bolton	2-1	1-1
Burnley	1-1	1-1
Charlton	2-3	3-0
Chelsea	3-2	2-0
Derby	5-0	2-4
Fulham	1-0	2-1
Huddersfield	1-0	1-1
Liverpool	2-3	1-1
Man City	1-2	1-1
Man United	2-0	0-2
Middlesbrough	3-1	1-2
Newcastle	2-1	2-7
Portsmouth	3-1	0-2
Preston	1-0	1-1
Stoke	2-0	6-1
Sunderland	2-0	1-0
West Brom	3-1	1-3
Wolves	4-2	1-1

Final League Record

P	W	D	L	F	A	Pts	Pos
42	22	9	11	76	51	53	2nd

FA Cup

Rnd 3	Scunthorpe Utd	(a)	3-0
Rnd 4	Newcastle Utd	(h)	0-3

the ball struck the referee before rebounding back to the grateful Baily, who seized upon the flat-footedness of the entire Huddersfield defence to sling over yet another cross. This time, Baily's centre found Len Duquemin and the Tottenham forward rose unchallenged to head past an amazed Jack Wheeler in the Huddersfield goal.

The reason for Huddersfield's inactivity was obvious. Under the laws of the game, Baily could not play the ball twice while taking a corner. Huddersfield's protests at losing a vital game 1-0 in such circumstances were understandable, but their efforts to have the result declared void came to naught and it was unfortunate that the scoreline probably sent them down to the Second Division. The arguments about the validity of the goal raged on. Did the referee consider himself to be a player when the ball struck him? If not — and it was an unlikely premise — the goal should have been disallowed and Huddersfield should have been awarded an indirect free kick. The only certain thing, of

◀ *Len Duquemin scored one of the most controversial goals in Spurs history when he headed home Eddie Baily's 'twice taken' free kick against Huddersfield to give Spurs a 1-0 win.*

Ted Ditchburn fails to stop West Brom scoring on the second Saturday of the 1951-2 season. But Spurs went on to win 3-1.
▼

In 1951-2, Tottenham Hotspur became First Division runners-up by the merest whisker, pipping close-neighbours Arsenal to the number two spot. Both sides finished on 53 points but Tottenham's goal average was 1·49 compared with Arsenal's 1·31. The top three placings read:

	P	W	D	L	F	A	Pts
Man United	42	23	11	8	95	52	57
Tottenham H	42	22	9	11	76	51	53
Arsenal	42	21	11	10	80	61	53

course, was that the Football League were not going to overrule the referee. Since that day, there have been other incidents, some televised, which have occasionally proved a referee to have erred. But the official reaction is that whatever the referee decides, must stand. It is a sound ruling, for any other stance would quickly lead to chaos. And referees are not wrong that often.

Thus fortifed by this good fortune, Spurs perhaps felt that the gods were at last on their side and if only their late run had started three games earlier, then they might have snatched the First Division title from under the noses of Manchester United who took it with fifty-seven points to Spurs fifty-three. But the writing was on the wall for this great Tottenham side and 1951-2 proved to be its last season of any great impact on the Football League.

1952-3

In 1952-3 it became abundantly clear that Arthur Rowe's brilliant 'push and run' team was, to phrase it perhaps a little unkindly, over the hill. The advance of years had caught up with some of the players who, after all, had started their careers as war clouds were gathering over Europe.

The partnership of Eddie Baily and Les Medley on the Tottenham left-wing — the left-wing that had seared a hole through most First Division defences in its day — was fading. The understanding which had taken them past whole sides with a series of deft, interchanging passes was not always there. And Billy Nicholson had lost his edge, too. Nicholson, one of the finest wing-halves ever to play for Tottenham Hotspur, had played a major part in the emergence of Alf Ramsey at full-back. Ramsey, fine player though he undoubtedly was, was slow to turn once a winger had passed him. It was Nicholson's uncanny ability to read the game which saved young Ramsey's face more than once. But now Nicholson, too, was not the young man he was and this had an adverse effect on his defensive colleague, although the pair of them were to play on with Spurs until 1954-5.

Most telling of all was the fact that Spurs had been 'rumbled' by their opponents. The Tottenham tactics no longer came as a shock to the other side and, like so many teams who have taken the game temporarily by storm with some new technique, the effectiveness of 'push and run', coupled with the collective ageing of the team, began to have its effect, although there were still occasions when Spurs flashed into life once more.

During 1952-3, Tottenham enjoyed a three-month unbeaten spell and Middlesbrough felt the full force of their anger and frustration at being unable to reproduce consistently, the football which had devastated other sides. At Ayrsome Park, Middlesbrough went down 4-0 to Spurs and at White Hart Lane Tottenham won 7-1. Blackpool were beaten 4-0 at home, Derby 5-2; and there was a spectacular 3-0 victory at Villa Park.

But there were dark days, too. Arsenal scored a double over Tottenham, scoring seven times in the two League matches between the two clubs, while Spurs could manage only one goal in reply. West Brom, Manchester United and Chelsea also won at White Hart Lane; and Tottenham lost twelve of their away matches and in fact won only thirteen points out of forty-two on opponents grounds. The side was going through a Jeykell and Hyde patch — on the wane but with patches of their old flair still showing through occasionally — and this was reflected in their final position of tenth place in the

Len Duquemin just evades a tackle from Birmingham City's Badham during the epic FA Cup quarter-final tussle between the two clubs.

Les Bennett is foiled by an opposing goalkeeper in a League match at White Hart Lane early in the 1952-3 season.

First Division with seventy-eight goals scored, but sixty-nine conceded.

Spurs final fall from the top came after their elimination from the FA Cup — although it seemed at one stage that they would march on to Wembley and yet another Cup Final. Poor Tranmere Rovers were the first side to get in Spurs way when they drew 1-1 on Merseyside, only to be ruthlessly removed 9-1 in the White Hart Lane replay the following week. Preston North End managed a 2-2 draw at Deepdale before Spurs beat them 1-0 when the teams met in London to move into the fifth round and a tie with Halifax Town of the Third Division (North) — a game which Spurs won 3-0 at The Shay in the most appalling conditions of ice and thick snow.

> *On their march to the FA Cup semi-final in 1952-3, Tottenham Hotspur played nine games (including four replays) and scored twenty-one goals with nine against. It was Spurs fifth semi-final.*

Birmingham City fought a 1-1 draw at St Andrews and a 2-2 draw at White Hart Lane before Sonny Walters scored a lone goal, late in the second replay to put Tottenham into the semi-final, where they met Blackpool, outright conquerors of Arsenal at Highbury in the sixth round. The two sides had met in the semi-final of 1947-8 when Blackpool won 3-1 at Villa Park. This season, Spurs were to do no better and with the scores level at 1-1, a mistake by

Alf Ramsey let Blackpool's Jackie Mudie in for the winner — again at Villa Park. While Blackpool went on to win the FA Cup in the historic 'Matthews Final' against Bolton Wanderers. Tottenham's season disintegrated completely. Only Len Duquemin — twenty-four League and Cup goals during 1952-3 — could feel reasonably satisfied. 'Push and run' was dying fast.

First Division results 1952-3

Arsenal	1-3	0-4
Aston Villa	1-1	3-0
Blackpool	4-0	0-2
Bolton	1-1	3-2
Burnley	2-1	2-3
Cardiff	2-1	0-0
Charlton	2-0	2-3
Chelsea	2-3	1-2
Derby	5-2	0-0
Liverpool	3-1	1-2
Man City	3-3	1-0
Man Utd	1-2	2-3
Middlesbrough	7-1	4-0
Newcastle	3-2	1-1
Portsmouth	3-3	1-2
Preston	4-4	0-1
Sheffield Wed	2-1	0-2
Stoke	1-0	0-2
Sunderland	2-2	1-1
West Brom	3-4	1-2
Wolves	3-2	0-0

Final League Record

P	W	D	L	F	A	Pts	Pos
42	15	11	16	78	69	41	10th

FA Cup

Rnd 3	Tranmere	(a)	1-1
Replay	Tranmere	(h)	9-1
Rnd 4	Preston	(a)	2-2
Replay	Preston	(h)	1-0
Rnd 5	Halifax	(a)	3-0
Rnd 6	Birmingham	(a)	1-1
Replay	Birmingham	(h)	2-2
2nd Replay	Birmingham	(n)	1-0
Semi-Final	Blackpool	(n)	1-2

1953-4

The close season of Coronation Year, 1953, saw the retirement of one Tottenham Hotspur left-winger and the debut of a new holder of the white number eleven shirt. While Les Medley hung up his boots and emigrated to Canada, George Robb, Finchley's amateur international and a schoolteacher, was persuaded to sign professional forms at White Hart Lane. But although he went on to win an England cap at full international level within three months of his first professional game, Robb could do little to prevent the final break-up of the 'push and run' side.

Tottenham started the season badly and it was evident that the gods were not to be with them on their journey through 1953-4. Although Rowe could see that the team which had achieved so much for Spurs was waning fast, there was a limit to what he could achieve in the time available. The season had started and the club needed new players in a bid to rebuild its side. But survival was the first priority, thus giving the Tottenham management time to consolidate.

> *Besides Alf Ramsey and George Robb, Spurs centre-half Harry Clarke was also capped by England in 1953-4. But like Robb – and Nicholson and Willis before him – Clarke made only one appearance. It was in England's 4-2 win over Scotland at Hampden Park on 3 April 1954. Compare this side with the one in which Robb had played earlier that season: Merrick; Staniforth, Byrne; Wright, Clarke, Dickinson; Finney, Broadis, Allen, Nicholls, Mullen.*

Spurs greatest asset — their tremendous rhythm and fluency — was gone. Each one of Tottenham's forty-two First Division matches was hard-fought and there were no forgone conclusions. Every one of the Spurs thirty-seven points was won and won hard — except perhaps a surprising 5-2 win at Huddersfield Town on a day when Tottenham recaptured some of their old flair. But overall, it was a bad season. Spurs lost exactly half their matches and won only sixteen, while their defensive record of seventy-six goals against was the worst Tottenham figure since they were relegated in 1934-5 (when ninety-three goals thundered into the Spurs net). In the final analysis, Spurs missed relegation by a comfortable seven points — Middlesbrough and Liverpool were the teams to go down to the Second Division — but sixteenth place was a big disappointment after the glories of the previous years.

Of all the Tottenham players that season, only one newly-signed George Robb really impressed. Robb won his first — and only — full England cap in the game against the Magical Magyars of Hungary at Wembley on 25 November 1953. It was a disastrous game for England. The Hungarians crushed them 6-3, with Alf Ramsey scoring one of England's goals from the penalty spot. The only England side in which Robb played is perhaps worth recalling. It was: Merrick; Ramsey, Eckersley; Wright, Johnston, Dickinson; Matthews, Taylor, Mortenson, Sewell, Robb. Robb was not alone in being blamed for the debacle. When England played Scotland at Hampden the following April, both full backs, the centre-half, and the entire England forward line had been chopped. Thus, Robb endured a similar fate to that of Bill Nicholson, who scored on his international debut against Portugal — within seconds of the kick-off at Goodison Park in May 1951 — and was never chosen again.

After being an ever-present since 1948-9 — and missing only one game in each of the seasons 1946-7 and 1947-8 — Spurs goalkeeper Ted Ditchburn's run of 247 consecutive games was broken during 1953-4 when he missed three matches through injury. A Tottenham team which did not start off with the name of Ditchburn seemed very strange indeed, and although he was to fight back and win three more England caps in 1956-7, Ditchburn, too, had seen his best days.

As so often happened when Tottenham Hotspur were doing less well in the First Division, it seemed

Spurs line-up for 1953-4. Skipper Ronnie Burgess (with ball) was fast coming to the end of his illustrious Tottenham career.

that the FA Cup might once again prove to be the saviour of the club's hopes, although two Second Division clubs both gave Tottenham a fright before they finally went out in the quarter-finals. In the third round Spurs travelled to Elland Road where Leeds held them to a 3-3 draw before losing the replay at White Hart Lane. Then, after Spurs had beaten Manchester City at Maine Road in the fourth round, Hull City managed a 1-1 draw at Hull before a single goal again saw off Yorkshire's Second Division challenge. Eventually, Spurs went out to West Brom, the team which went on to win the Cup that season and finish second in the First Division. Tottenham Hotspur ended the 1953-4 season with the knowledge that intensive team rebuilding had to be done before they could face the following campaign with any confidence.

FA Cup

Rnd 3	Leeds Utd	(a)	3-3
Replay	Leeds Utd	(h)	1-0
Rnd 4	Man City	(a)	1-0
Rnd 5	Hull City	(a)	1-1
Replay	Hull City	(h)	1-0
Rnd 6	West Brom	(a)	0-3

Bill Nicholson (far right) sees a shot graze the Newcastle United post during Spurs 3-0 win over the Magpies in February 1954.

First Division results 1953-4

	H	A
Arsenal	1-4	3-0
Aston Villa	1-0	2-1
Blackpool	2-2	0-1
Bolton	3-2	0-2
Burnley	2-3	2-4
Cardiff	0-1	0-1
Charlton	3-1	1-0
Chelsea	2-1	0-1
Huddersfield	1-0	5-2
Liverpool	2-1	2-2
Man City	3-0	1-4
Man United	1-1	0-2
Middlesbrough	4-1	0-3
Newcastle	3-0	3-1
Portsmouth	1-1	1-1
Preston	2-6	1-2
Sheffield Utd	2-1	2-5
Sheffield Wed	3-1	1-2
Sunderland	0-3	3-4
West Brom	0-1	0-3
Wolves	2-3	0-2

Final League Record

P	W	D	L	F	A	Pts	Pos
42	16	5	21	65	76	37	16th

1954-5

Season 1954-5 was one of complete transition for Tottenham Hotspur. Bill Nicholson and Alf Ramsey played their last games for Spurs, while Tottenham signed a player who was to become one of the most famous names in the club's history. Danny Blanchflower had become increasingly disenchanted with Aston Villa, the club that had signed him from Barnsley, and the Irish international wing-half became the target of both Arsenal and Spurs as the 1954-5 season got underway. Arsenal decided that £28,500 was as far as they would go; but Tottenham, to their eternal credit, decided that they would keep in the race for the Irishman's signature and at £30,000, Spurs got their man.

It was perhaps inevitable that Blanchflower would find himself at Spurs anyway. A cultured, thinking footballer who had returned from a visit to Canada with the Northern Ireland team, full of an exciting new defensive system that he had seen a Swiss team use, and which he was convinced would suit Villa, only to see it fall on deaf ears, Blanchflower was attracted by the Spurs style and reputation for thoughtful football.

Shortly after Rowe had signed the man he saw as the logical successor to Nicholson at wing-half and Ramsey as skipper, the Tottenham manager fell ill and was replaced by assistant manager Jimmy Anderson. Blanchflower had just made his First Division debut for Tottenham in the goalless draw against Manchester City at Maine Road in December but sadly, the man who was responsible for bringing him to White Hart Lane, would not have the immense pleasure of working with the man who was to help bring Spurs back to the top again.

Burgess and Willis had joined Swansea Town but in the other direction had come Mel Hopkins, the player who was to win thirty-four full international caps for Wales. Johnny Brooks, a skilful inside-forward from Reading, and goalkeeper Ron Reynolds from Aldershot were other new names who were to figure increasingly in the Tottenham Hotspur line-up. Len Duquemin's place, for so long impregnable, was given up to Dave Dumore from York City. One era had ended. Another was about to begin.

> *Spurs did almost as well on opponents' grounds as they did at White Hart Lane in 1954-5. Out of their forty points, no less than eighteen were won away from home (seven wins and four draws). It was an away record of which many more successful clubs would have been proud.*

Tottenham Hotspur's immediate fortunes were not all that clear, however, and several times during 1953-4 Spurs hovered around the relegation zone and looked more likely to drop back into the Second Division than to be on the way to recapturing some of their old glory days. Indeed, at one stage of the season, Spurs were in twenty-first place in the First Division. In the FA Cup there was also humiliation on the way, although Tottenham could

not have had an easier path to what should have been the quarter-finals. First, Spurs met Third Division (North) side, Gateshead at Redheugh Park and beat the North-East minnows 2-0. Then Third Division (South) team Port Vale came to White Hart Lane and were beaten 4-2. The previous season, Vale had shocked all football by reaching the FA Cup semi-finals before losing to West Brom, the team which had knocked Spurs out of the previous round.

Having disposed of the previous season's giant-killers, Spurs had no reason to fear York City when they were drawn to play at Bootham Crescent in the fifth round on 19 February. But York were to take up where Port Vale left off and Spurs went down 3-1 to a York side containing such characters as the redoubtable Arthur Bottom. That York themselves were beaten in the semi-finals by Newcastle United, the eventual winners, was no consolation to Tottenham.

For the second successive season, Spurs lost more league games than they won and after the Cup defeat by little York City, the side found it increasingly difficult to pick themselves up. Eventually Spurs finished with three more points than the previous campaign, although they failed to improve on six-teenth place. But there were flashes of better times to come and, after all, the Tottenham side was under-going fairly major surgery. Big home wins over the two Sheffield clubs — Wednesday went down 7-2 and United 5-0 — and a 5-1 home defeat of Leicester City, all helped Tottenham fans to have hope that better days were round the corner. The embryo of another great Tottenham team was emerging. With Ramsey on his way to Ipswich Town and Baily to Port Vale, Bill Nicholson became the club coach as Tottenham began again.

Northern Ireland international wing-half Danny Blanch-flower joined Spurs from Aston Villa. Before long he would become one of the most popular players at White Hart Lane.

First Division results 1954-5

	H	A
Arsenal	0-1	0-2
Aston Villa	1-1	4-2
Blackpool	3-2	1-5
Bolton	2-0	2-1
Burnley	0-3	2-1
Cardiff	0-2	2-1
Charlton	1-4	2-1
Chelsea	2-4	1-2
Everton	1-3	0-1
Huddersfield	1-1	0-1
Leicester	5-1	0-2
Man City	2-2	0-0
Man United	0-2	1-2
Newcastle	2-1	4-4
Portsmouth	1-1	3-0
Preston	3-1	0-1
Sheffield Utd	5-0	1-4
Sheffield Wed	7-2	2-2
Sunderland	0-1	1-1
West Brom	3-1	2-1
Wolves	3-2	2-4

Final League Record

P	W	D	L	F	A	Pts	Pos
42	16	8	18	72	73	40	16th

FA Cup

Rnd 3	Gateshead	(a)	2-0
Rnd 4	Port Vale	(h)	4-2
Rnd 5	York City	(a)	1-3

Ron Reynolds took over Ted Ditchburn's place in the Spurs first team.

1955-6

Tottenham Hotspur fans had to undergo one more almost disastrous season in 1955-6 before the new Tottenham blend took their club to new honours. In that season, Spurs were almost continually fighting to avoid relegation and in the end they did so by just two points. That was the slender margin which separated Tottenham Hotspur from the relegated club Huddersfield Town who finished in twenty-first place.

There were still more new faces on the Tottenham staff. Maurice Norman was signed from Norwich City to replace Alf Ramsey who had played his last league game for Tottenham; bustling centre-forward Bobby Smith came to White Hart Lane from London neighbours, Chelsea; and the names of Peter Baker and Ron Henry — soon to become legendary full-backs in a great Spurs side — were making an impression; finally, the diminutive Terry Dyson was also making the first team.

But if the First Division survival kit was only just adequate enough to save Spurs from the feared drop, then once again the name of Tottenham Hotspur blazed a trail in the FA Cup. Mindful of their shock Cup exit at the hands of York City the previous season, Spurs were in no mood for levity when they drew Midland League side Boston United in the third round. Boston, complete with six ex-Derby players, had just beaten Derby County 6-1 at the Baseball Ground! Tottenham beat Boston 4-0 at White Hart Lane — although the Lincolnshire club's right-winger, Reg Harrison, who had won an FA Cup-winners medal with Derby in 1946, was adamant that Boston should have been two goals up before Spurs scored. But then, the FA Cup is full of glorious 'ifs' and 'buts'.

Spurs missed relegation by the skin of their teeth in 1955-6. Here are the bottom five clubs and their records:

	P	W	D	L	F	A	Pts
Tottenham	*42*	*15*	*7*	*20*	*61*	*71*	*37*
Preston	*42*	*14*	*8*	*20*	*73*	*72*	*36*
Aston Villa	*42*	*11*	*13*	*18*	*52*	*69*	*35*
Huddersfield	*42*	*14*	*7*	*21*	*54*	*83*	*35*
Sheffield Utd	*42*	*12*	*9*	*21*	*63*	*77*	*33*

Spurs progressed further. They beat Middlesbrough 3-1 and Doncaster Rovers 2-0, before meeting old rivals West Ham United in the sixth round at White Hart Lane. With the Hammers leading by a goal, and with minutes ticking away, Spurs skipper Danny Blanchflower decided on a bold tactical move. He pushed Maurice Norman — signed as a full-back but now playing at centre-half — forward into the Tottenham attack and the gamble paid off. Spurs equalised and with the final score at 3-3 they went to Upton Park and won the replay 2-1 to enter the semi-finals.

With the prospect of an FA Cup Final appearance looming up, it occurred to Spurs fans that, although their club had won the Cup twice, they had never played in a Wembley Final. And they had to look back over thirty years to 1921 for Tottenham's last success. Manager Jimmy Anderson sprang a surprise before the semi-final against Manchester City at Villa Park when he dropped Tommy Harmer, the outside-right who had played so very well in the games leading up to the last-four stage. Alas, Spurs were to wait a little while longer to play in the FA Cup Final at Wembley. Manchester City's Bobby Johnstone scored to put his side in front and although Blanchflower again gambled with Norman pushed up into the attack, the ploy this time came to nothing and the score line remained unaltered as Spurs dipped out once again. Blanchflower, the hero and genius of the West Ham

Another name that was to become a Spurs legend was to make the first team in 1955-6 – Terry Dyson.

Ron Reynolds tips over a Sheffield United shot during the First Division match at White Hart Lane.

tie, was now called a few other names by the Tottenham directors and he finished the season no longer captain. It was another example of the fickleness of football. Norman's inclusion in the attack had not weakened Spurs defence for City failed to score again; and yet because it had failed to produce a goal at the other end, questions were asked.

Nevertheless, the FA Cup run of 1955-6 served to give the Tottenham team some kind of momentum. Although they struggled in the First Division — gaining only thirty-seven points to finish in eighteenth place — the successes of the Cup were obvious signs that the team was emerging as one which would fight its way back to the top of the table. George Robb was still playing on the left-wing and with the newer players finding their feet, the stage was set for a revival of quite staggering proportions the following season.

Ted Ditchburn played in fourteen First Division games in 1955-6 but, just as the following season was to be a new beginning for the club, so it would prove to be the re-birth — albeit brief — of Ditchburn's career, even to the extent of winning further caps. For Spurs one and all, 1955-6 would be the last dark period for quite some time.

FA Cup

Rnd 3	Boston United	(h)	4-0
Rnd 4	Middlesbrough	(h)	3-1
Rnd 5	Doncaster Rov	(a)	2-0
Rnd 6	West Ham Utd	(h)	3-3
Replay	West Ham Utd	(a)	2-1
Semi-final	Man City	(n)	0-1

First Division results 1955-6

	H	A
Arsenal	3-1	1-0
Aston Villa	4-3	2-0
Birmingham	0-1	0-3
Blackpool	1-1	2-0
Bolton	0-3	2-3
Burnley	0-1	0-2
Cardiff	1-1	0-0
Charlton	2-3	2-1
Chelsea	4-0	0-2
Everton	1-1	1-2
Huddersfield	1-2	0-1
Luton	2-1	1-2
Man City	2-1	2-1
Man Utd	1-2	2-2
Newcastle	3-1	2-1
Portsmouth	1-1	1-4
Preston	0-4	3-3
Sheffield Utd	3-1	0-2
Sunderland	2-3	2-3
West Brom	4-1	0-1
Wolves	2-1	1-5

Final League Record

P	W	D	L	F	A	Pts	Pos
42	15	7	20	61	71	37	18th

1956-7

All Tottenham Hotspur's hopes were fulfilled in 1956-7. True, no trophies actually finished up in the White Hart Lane Boardroom, but Spurs were on the way back, although their final runners-up spot in the First Division was some eight points behind the champions, Manchester United.

In league matches Tottenham lost only eight games and increased their goalscoring power to the tune of 104 goals — an average of nearly 2·5 per game. The defence tightened up as well and Tottenham's rearguard conceded only fifty-six goals, which was a big improvement on the previous season.

The Tottenham goals for were equally shared. Bobby Smith and Alf Stokes — who displaced Johnny Brookes from the Spurs first team — each scored eighteen, while Tommy Harmer hit seventeen. Harmer was not noted for his goalscoring and it was one of the surprises of the season that he should find the net so many times. With George Robb and Terry Medwin each scoring fourteen goals, seventy-eight per cent of Spurs goals had been found by just five players.

Spurs ran Manchester United close for much of the season and in fact, the two matches between the sides both ended all-square — 2-2 at White Hart Lane and 0-0 at Old Trafford. Only in the final run in to the season did United at last pull away to finish quite convincing champions. Naturally, with a total in excess of three figures, Spurs enjoyed some big wins in 1956-7. Everton were beaten 6-0 at home and Charlton hammered 6-2 at White Hart Lane. In addition, Birmingham, Cardiff, Leeds, Luton and Sunderland all came to London and had five goals rammed past them.

Even away from home, while not finding the net

Spurs team 1956-7. Tommy Harmer (with the ball) surprised everyone by scoring seventeen goals.

so regularly, Spurs lost only six games out of twenty-one. The only side to do the double over them was Arsenal. The Gunners won both games 3-1 to win the unofficial 'championship' of North London, even if they finished in eventual fifth place, six points behind their old rivals, Spurs.

Spurs checkered career in the FA Cup continued. Two seasons before they had knocked out giant-killers, Port Vale, and then themselves been knocked out by Third Division York City. Then, Spurs had fought their way to the semi-final in 1955-6; now, in 1956-7 Tottenham were to provide the latest victims for the current FA Cup giantkillers, Bournemouth and Boscombe Athletic, managed by an old Spurs player, Freddie Cox.

Tottenham had beaten Leicester City and Chelsea, both at home, to reach the fifth round, while Bournemouth had started off in the first round with an easy tie and then through the second to the third stage where they were disappointed to draw — not one of the First Division clubs who come in at that stage — but fellow Third Division side Accrington Stanley from the Northern Section. Bournemouth took advantage of this by winning 2-0 and then in the fifth round their prayers were answered when they drew Wolves at Molineux. A broken goalpost added to the drama as Wolves went down 1-0 and brought Tottenham Hotspur to the South Coast and a tricky fifth round tie at Dean Court. It was a test which proved too much for Tottenham on the day. Bournemouth won 3-1 to earn a sixth round tie with none other than Manchester United (when they were beaten just 2-1). When Spurs had lost to York they had been struggling. The defeat by Bournemouth was a major shock.

But Spurs were a force to be reckoned with again. Ditchburn, although being dropped in favour of Ron Reynolds after the Bournemouth humiliation, had already added three more England caps when he appeared against Wales and Yugoslavia in November, and against Denmark in December. England won all three games and Ditchburn conceded only three goals. After he lost his Spurs place, Ditchburn naturally lost his England spot as well.

Johnny Brooks also played for England three times — in the same matches as Ditchburn — and although he scored in two of them, he, too, paid the price of not being a regular in the Spurs first team. Mel Hopkins and Terry Medwin (Wales) and Danny Blanchflower (Northern Ireland) also represented their country in 1956-7. International representation of this calibre was another sign that Tottenham Hotspur were on the upward trail.

From eighteenth place to second in twelve months – that was Spurs achievement in 1956-7. Here are the top positions in the first Division table.

	P	W	D	L	F	A	Pts
Man United	42	28	8	6	103	54	64
Tottenham	42	22	12	8	104	56	56
Preston	42	23	10	9	84	56	56
Blackpool	42	22	9	11	93	65	53
Arsenal	42	21	8	13	85	69	50
Wolves	42	20	8	14	94	70	48

Final League Record

P	W	D	L	F	A	Pts	Pos
42	22	12	8	104	56	56	2nd

FA Cup

Rnd 3	Leicester	(h)	2-0
Rnd 4	Chelsea	(h)	4-0
Rnd 5	Bournemouth	(a)	1-3

First Division results 1956-7

	H	A
Arsenal	1-3	1-3
Aston Villa	3-0	4-2
Birmingham	5-1	0-0
Blackpool	2-1	1-4
Bolton	4-0	0-1
Burnley	2-0	0-1
Cardiff	5-0	3-0
Charlton	6-2	1-1
Chelsea	3-4	4-2
Everton	6-0	1-1
Leeds	5-1	1-1
Luton	5-0	3-1
Man City	3-2	2-2
Man United	2-2	0-0
Newcastle	3-1	2-2
Portsmouth	2-0	3-2
Preston	1-1	4-1
Sheffield Wed.	1-1	1-4
Sunderland	5-2	2-0
West Brom	2-2	1-1
Wolves	4-1	0-3

Bobby Smith, seen here in the 3-2 win against Manchester City, scored eighteen goals in 1956-7.

1957-8

On the first day of the 1957-8 season, Tottenham Hotspur fans had much to look forward to, as their rejuvenated team set out for the First Division championship which they had come close to taking the previous season. Spurs first match of the new season was at White Hart Lane and their opponents were Chelsea, so often the butt of music hall jokes despite the fact that they had taken the title in 1955.

A London derby match was always an event and for the Tottenham supporters, this early clash with the Stamford Bridge side provided a sound opportunity for Spurs to get away to a cracking start. Chelsea, after all, had finished only twelfth in 1956-7 and could not be expected to prove all that difficult an obstacle for Spurs to remove on the way to a home win.

But Chelsea had a certain young player making his debut for them that day. His name was Jimmy Greaves and as a Chelsea junior, he had scored an incredible 100 goals the previous season. Jimmy Greaves, of course, was to go on to remarkable achievements, including scoring a goal on his debut for every team in which he played. And the first day of the 1957-8 season was no exception. Greaves began his astonishing career with a goal at White Hart Lane and although Tottenham managed to finish the match level at 1-1, it was an unhappy start. A point dropped at home against old rivals was not the best way to kick off a new season — especially a season in which everyone thought that the team would take the title.

Jimmy Iley who came from Sheffield United to replace Tony Marchi at wing-half in the Spurs team.

Tottenham's final position of third in 1957-8 was perhaps not as impressive as it first appears. Here are the top positions:

	P	W	D	L	F	A	Pts
Wolves	42	28	8	6	103	47	64
Preston	42	26	7	9	100	51	59
Tottenham	42	21	9	12	93	77	51
West Brom	42	18	14	10	92	70	50
Man City	42	22	5	15	104	100	49

Things did not immediately improve, either. Tottenham were beaten 5-1 at Portsmouth and 3-1 at Newcastle before Portsmouth came back to White Hart Lane and completed a double with a 5-3 victory. Yet, incredibly, at the end of the season, with Spurs safely in third place, it was Portsmouth who missed relegation only on goal average.

The man most responsible for Tottenham overcoming this poor start to the season to finish a creditable third in the table — albeit thirteen points behind champions Wolves and eight adrift of runners up Preston North End — was Danny Blanchflower. Blanchflower coaxed and schemed Tottenham to better things and his skill and tactical knowledge was recognised by the game's writers when he was elected Footballer of the Year.

Spurs finished the season with ninety-three goals in league matches and bustling Bobby Smith — the man they had signed from Chelsea — signalled his arrival as a First Division marksman with thirty-six of those goals, equalling the club's individual scoring record set up by Ted Harper. In all teams of great skill, there has to be one player whose determination and courage capitalises on the fine works of other players. Smith was such a performer.

On the debit side, though, there were failures in 1957-8. Both Alf Stokes and Johnny Brooks had more mediocre games than they had good ones and with George Robb a passenger for much of the time because of a painful knee injury — Robb bravely played in many games which he could well have missed — there was good reason for Jimmy Anderson to look around for replacements. Anderson found one such replacement at Swansea Town and the player he signed went on to become a great Spur, although at first it looked likely that Anderson had wasted the club's money. But Cliff Jones was to recover from a mediocre start to give Tottenham fans some of the most dazzling exhibitions of wing play they had ever seen. Coupled with his flair for scoring goals, Jones repaid Tottenham's fee and Anderson's faith in him, many times over.

Another new Spurs signing in 1957-8 was wing-half Jim Iley, who came from Sheffield United to replace Tony Marchi, Spurs England 'B' player who had gone to Italy, lured by tales of the huge fortunes which players could earn in the land of the lira. In the FA Cup, Spurs enjoyed an easy enough win over Leicester City in the third round — but when Sheffield United came to White Hart Lane in the fourth round, Iley could tell his new teammates nothing about his old club which proved to be of any use — and United surprisingly won 3-0.

Freed — if that is the right word — of Cup involvement, Tottenham battled on for a First Division title which they might well have thought to be theirs before the season started. But that poor start was hanging round their necks like a millstone and Spurs were never in serious contention. In the end, third place was more than Spurs fans dared have hoped for after a month of the season. But it was where their club finally finished — thanks to the mastery of Danny Blanchflower.

First Division results 1957-8

	H	A
Arsenal	3-1	4-4
Aston Villa	6-2	1-1
Birmingham	7-1	0-0
Blackpool	2-1	2-0
Bolton	4-1	2-3
Burnley	3-1	0-2
Chelsea	1-1	4-2
Everton	3-1	4-3
Leeds	2-0	2-1
Leicester	1-4	3-1
Luton	3-1	0-0
Man City	5-1	1-5
Man United	1-0	4-3
Newcastle	3-3	1-3
Nottm Forest	3-4	2-1
Portsmouth	3-5	1-5
Preston	3-3	1-3
Sheffield	4-2	0-2
Sunderland	0-1	1-1
West Brom	0-0	2-0
Wolves	1-0	0-4

Final League Record

P	W	D	L	F	A	Pts	Pos
42	21	9	12	93	77	51	3rd

FA Cup

Rnd 3	Leicester	(h)	4-0
Rnd 4	Sheffield U	(h)	0-3

Cliff Jones recovered from a mediocre start to give Spurs years of service and repay many times over his transfer fee from Swansea Town.

1958-9

Two games sum up the 1958-9 season for Tottenham Hotspur. One was a highlight, the other a low point. And that was how the season went, with Spurs finally finishing in eighteenth place, being knocked out of the FA Cup by a Third Division side, losing a stalwart name who had been associated with the club since the war, and changing managers in mid-stream.

The name to leave Tottenham after many years of glorious service was Ted Ditchburn. Ditchburn played his 418th league game for Tottenham against Chelsea early in the season, broke his finger, and went off to become player-manager of Romford, while John Hollowbread took his place. One of the last links with Spurs 'push and run' side had been severed.

Then came the appointment of Bill Nicholson as manager. Nicholson had coached Tottenham since he retired as a player and in the summer of 1958 he had been assistant to the England team manager Walter Winterbottom in the World Cup in Sweden. He replaced Jimmy Anderson as manager with the season just a few weeks old and his first game in charge was destined to bring a result beyond the wildest dreams of a man taking his first step into full managership of a First Division side.

On 11 October 1958, Spurs were due to play a league match against Everton at White Hart Lane. Apart from the fans of the two clubs, no-one else singled the match out for special attention. In London, Chelsea were at home to Bolton Wanderers and West Ham United entertained Birmingham City. Spurs were sixteenth in the table with nine points from their eleven games; Everton were twentieth. Yet the game was to be one of the most famous of all time.

In only the second minute, Alf Stokes cracked home a rebound and Spurs were 1-0 ahead; eight minutes later Everton were level 1-1 when Jim Harris diverted Dave Hickson's cross; minutes later, Spurs regained their one-goal advantage when Bobby Smith steered Harmer's pass past Albert Dunlop in the Everton goal. It was fast and furious stuff, but after thirty minutes the game was still finely balanced. Three Spurs goals in four minutes changed all that! Harmer sent Robb away on a mazy dribble and the winger made it 3-1; Blanchflower centred precisely for Smith to score the fourth; and after Dunlop could only parry Robb's header, Stokes ran it to make it 5-1. When Medwin scored via an Everton post to make the scoreline 6-1 just before half-time, the crowd was alight with excitement.

Danny Blanchflower and Bobby Collins tangle during the astonishing 10-4 Spurs victory over Everton at White Hart Lane.

From the restart, Everton pulled a goal back when Harris headed home Fielding's corner. But any hopes of a spectacular recovery were soon dimmed when Smith headed home to make it 7-2. It often happens that a big half-time score is not added to greatly in the second half, and with only ten minutes left and the score still 7-2 it looked as though this had happened again — a big win, but not that spectacular. Then it all started again. Harmer made it 8-2 for Spurs and Harris completed his hat-trick for Everton, before Smith scored his fourth and Spurs ninth to make the score 9-3. But still the match had not ended. Bobby Collins blasted a 25-yarder past Hollowbread to make it an amazing 9-4; and then Spurs reached double-figures when Ryden hammered the tenth and final goal past the hapless Everton goalkeeper. How did it all happen? No-one can say. It was just one of those freak days when every shot went home. It was left to Tommy Harmer — who had a superb match — to say to Nicholson as the players left the field 'We won't score ten every week, boss!'.

> *Tottenham's team for that epic 10-4 win over Everton on 11 October 1958 was: Hollowbread; Baker, Hopkins; Blanchflower, Ryden, Iley; Medwin, Harmer, Smith, Stokes, Robb. Incredibly, only Blanchflower, Baker and Smith were regular members of the Spurs side which did the historic 'double' two seasons later.*

At the other end of the scale Tottenham were knocked out of the FA Cup by Norwich City in 1958-9, when the Third Division (South) club reached the sixth round (and went on to lose to Luton Town in the semi-final) by beating Spurs 1-0 at Carrow Road after the two sides had drawn 1-1 at White Hart Lane. In the sixty-third minute of the replay, ace scorer Terry Bly drove the ball past Hollowbread and the Canaries were home.

Spurs finished the season in eighteenth place, missing relegation by six points. It had been a strange campaign. Before it started, Cliff Jones broke a leg in training; then Jimmy Anderson's illness had forced his retirement after fifty years outstanding service. Then Nicholson's era had begun. It was to be one of the most glorious in Spurs history.

First Division results 1958-9

	H	A
Arsenal	1-4	1-3
Aston Villa	3-2	1-1
Birmingham	0-4	1-5
Blackburn	3-1	0-5
Blackpool	2-3	0-0
Bolton	1-1	1-4
Burnley	2-2	1-3
Chelsea	4-0	2-4
Everton	10-4	1-2
Leeds	2-3	1-3
Leicester	6-0	4-3
Luton	3-0	2-1
Man City	3-1	1-5
Man United	1-3	2-2
Newcastle	1-3	2-1
Nottm Forest	1-0	1-1
Portsmouth	4-4	1-1
Preston	1-2	2-2
West Brom	5-0	3-4
West Ham	1-4	1-2
Wolves	2-1	1-1

Final League Record

P	W	D	L	F	A	Pts	Pos
42	13	10	19	85	95	36	18th

FA Cup

Rnd 3	West Ham Utd	(h)	2-0
Rnd 4	Newport Co (h)	(h)	4-1
Rnd 5	Norwich City	(h)	1-1
Replay	Norwich City	(a)	0-1

Spurs team which did service during 1958-9. Goalkeeper John Hollowbread replaced long-serving Ted Ditchburn who went to non-League Romford.

1959-60

Bill Nicholson's 'double'-winning Spurs team was already taking shape. In March 1959, Nicholson had signed lion-hearted Dave Mackay from Heart of Midlothian for £30,000 — despite scares in the press that Mackay had 'a weak leg'. In the close season he brought another Scottish international to White Hart Lane with the purchase of Dundee's goalkeeper Bill Brown. And that same scorching summer, Nicholson also re-signed Tony Marchi from Juventus. The former Spur was yet another English exile aching to get back home.

During the season, other players were added. The notable one was John White, who Nicholson snapped up from Falkirk for a fee reported to be as low as £20,000. Les Allen came from Chelsea with Johnny Brooks going to Stamford Bridge; and John Smith of West Ham changed places with Dave Dunmore as Nicholson brought together the nucleus of the side which would make football history.

It was another poor start which cost Tottenham the championship in 1959-60. Although they played thirteen games without defeat, and despite the fact that teams like Newcastle and Manchester United were beaten 5-1 away from home, Spurs dropped home points with a succession of drawn matches at White Hart Lane and at Easter 1960, successive home reverses at the hands of Manchester City and Chelsea — who both came to White Hart Lane and won 1-0 — finally killed their chances of the First Division title.

The final placings in 1959-60s First Division championship race were extremely close. The top four clubs were:	P	W	D	L	F	A	Pts
Burnley	42	24	7	11	85	61	55
Wolves	42	24	6	12	106	67	54
Tottenham	42	21	11	10	86	50	53
West Brom	42	19	11	12	83	57	49

The Manchester City victory centred around a controversial penalty which Spurs missed and which would have levelled the scores and — who knows...? Cliff Jones took the kick but City's Bert Trautmann, the famous German prisoner-of-war, saved it but could not stop Jones from following up to hammer the ball home, only to see the referee disallow the goal because he said time had run out.

The arguments raged that the referee could not possibly time the match to such a precise degree. Yet he had already extended the forty-five minutes to allow the first kick to be taken and so he was probably right in his ruling, although Tottenham's players and fans were far from convinced. The Chelsea goal which sunk Spurs was scored — inevitably — by Jimmy Greaves.

Spurs won 3-1 at Wolverhampton and beat Blackpool 4-1 at White Hart Lane to finish in third spot and curiously, their win over Wolves cost the Molineux club the precious League and Cup 'double' which Spurs themselves were to take the following year. On a warm, sunny day in April 1960, 55,000 fan packed into the Wolves ground to see their team try to complete the first leg of the double. They topped the First Division with fifty-two points from forty games; Spurs were second with forty-nine from the same number; and Burnley were third with forty-eight points, but from only thirty-eight matches. Wolves must win. After only two minutes Blanchflower and Jones combined and Blanchflower swung over an inch-perfect centre which Bobby Smith crashed past Malcolm Finlayson.

Although Peter Broadbent equalised for Wolves when Bill Brown could not hold his first shot, Spurs were back in front before half-time when Dave Mackay — playing at inside-left in place of the injured Les Allen — headed home a cross from Bobby Smith after the centre-forward had wandered out to the wing. When Spurs scored again through Jones, who launched himself at a low cross and headed home the third goal, Wolves were down and out. Alas, Spurs could not hold off the challenge of Burnley and the Lancashire club took the title.

In the FA Cup Spurs had scored a staggering thirteen goals against Third Division (North) strugglers Crewe after the Cheshire side held Tottenham to a 2-2 draw at Gresty Road. In the next round — the fifth — Spurs were beaten 3-1 by Blackburn Rovers. It would be over two seasons before Tottenham lost another FA Cup-tie.

FA Cup

Rnd 3	Newport Co	(a)	4-0
Rnd 4	Crewe Alex	(a)	2-2
Replay	Crew Alex	(h)	13-2
Rnd 5	Blackburn	(h)	1-3

Cliff Jones rounds a Preston defender on the way to Tottenham's 5-1 win over the Lancashire club in September 1959.

John White joined Spurs from Falkirk for £20,000.

First Division results 1959-60

	H	A
Arsenal	3-0	1-1
Birmingham	0-0	1-0
Blackburn	2-1	4-1
Blackpool	4-1	2-2
Bolton	0-2	1-2
Burnley	1-1	0-2
Chelsea	0-1	3-1
Everton	3-0	1-2
Fulham	1-1	1-1
Leeds	1-4	4-2
Leicester	1-2	1-1
Luton	1-1	0-1
Man City	0-1	2-1
Man Utd	2-1	5-1
Newcastle	4-0	5-1
Nottm Forest	2-1	3-1
Preston	5-1	1-1
Sheffield Wed	4-1	1-2
West Brom	2-2	2-1
West Ham	2-2	2-1
Wolves	5-1	3-1

Final League Record

P	W	D	L	F	A	Pts	Pos
42	21	11	10	86	50	53	3rd

1960-1

There was never much doubt that Spurs would win the Football League championship in 1960-1 — and in the final analysis there was never much doubt that they would become the first team in modern times to win the historic 'double' of League and Cup.

From the moment Les Allen and Bobby Smith gave Spurs a 2-0 win over Everton at White Hart Lane on the opening day of the season, Spurs staked their claim to the title of Team of the Century with a fantastic opening run of eleven successive wins which is still unequalled in the history of the Football League. Even a 1-1 draw at home to Manchester City was followed by a further four wins before Spurs slipped to their first defeat in their seventeenth match of the season.

By the time they went to Hillsborough on 12 November, Spurs had dropped just one point and scored fifty-three goals. It was an incredible performance and even defeat at the hands of Sheffield Wednesday did nothing to hide the fact that Tottenham had opened up such a gap at the top of the First Division that only a major disaster would prevent them from galloping away with the title. Many superlatives have been heaped upon this now legendary team. But quite simply, they were immaculate. When they beat Nottingham Forest 4-0 at the City Ground on 15 October 1960, *The People* reporter whose job it was to award merit marks, just threw up his hands in admiration and gave every Spurs player on the field ten out of ten.

Spurs did not let that first defeat at Sheffield worry them. After all, no matter how brilliant a team was, it was inevitable that they would go down once or twice over a forty-two-match programme.

When West Ham visited White Hart Lane on Christmas Eve 1960, Spurs stood proudly at the top of the First Division where they had been since the first week of the season. They had forty points from twenty-two matches — a deficit of only four points. The Hammers were no match for their London rivals. White and Dyson were on hand to help Spurs to yet another win. Two days later at Upton Park, Spurs won the return match 3-0, and on New Year's Eve, they put the seal on the first half of the season with a 5-2 drubbing of Blackburn Rovers.

Over two million people watched Tottenham Hotspur in 1960-1. The goalscorers in this epic season were: League: Smith 28, Allen 23, Jones 15, White 13, Dyson 12, Blanchflower 6, Medwin 5, Mackay 4, Norman 4, Saul 3, Baker 1, opposition own goal 1
FA Cup: Dyson 5, Smith 5, Allen 4, Jones 4, Mackay 2, opposition own goal 1

On the first Saturday of 1961, Spurs put aside their relentless drive for the title and turned their attention to the FA Cup. They moved sweetly through to the fourth round with a 3-2 win over Charlton.

Back to League action and Spurs suffered their second defeat of the season when Manchester United won 2-0 at Old Trafford. One week later Arsenal were comprehensively beaten and on 8 January, Crewe Alexandra came back to London to face Spurs in the Cup. What thoughts must have been going through the Crewe players' minds we can only imagine. Twelve months earlier they had been crushed 13-2 at White Hart Lane. This time, Spurs were in the mood for compromise and Crewe escaped with a 5-1 thrashing. A 3-2 home defeat by Leicester followed, but these rare setbacks were now academic. Spurs became the first side ever to reach fifty points from as few as twenty-nine games.

Aston Villa fell in the Cup and then Sunderland had the temerity to hold Spurs 1-1 at Roker Park in the sixth round before being slammed 5-0 in the following midweek replay. A week before the semi-

Double winners. Spurs with the FA Cup and Football League Championship Trophy. Back row (left to right): Brown, Baker, Henry, Blanchflower, Norman, Mackay. Front: Jones, White, Smith, Allen, Dyson. They were the first team this century to take the 'double'.

final, Spurs had lost 3-2 at Cardiff but they always seemed to bounce back from a rare defeat by becoming even more invincible. Burnley had to be content to play a supporting role in the semi-final at Villa Park where two goals from Bobby Smith clinched Tottenham Hotspur a place at Wembley. Although Burnley scored a surprise win in the League on the penultimate Saturday of the season, the championship already belonged to Tottenham. When Spurs stepped out into the Wembley sunshine on 6 May 1961, the 100,000 crowd sensed they were about to see history made.

Spurs had come this far — they would not fall now. Terry Dyson gave them the lead and Leicester City were as good as beaten. Late in the second half, Bobby Smith made it 2-0 and skipper Danny Blanchflower glanced up at the Wembley scoreboard for the first time to confirm to himself that he was part of history in the making. Spurs became the first team since Aston Villa in 1897 to win both trophies in the same season. But Spurs achievement was infinitely greater. They had played many more games than Villa — and in a fiercely competitive league.

Leicester goalkeeper Gordon Banks fails to stop Bobby Smith scoring Spurs second goal during the 1961 FA Cup Final.

Leicester defenders breathe a sigh of relief as a Dyson header grazes the crossbar.

First Division results 1960-1

	H	A
Arsenal	4-2	3-2
Aston Villa	6-2	2-1
Birmingham	6-0	3-2
Blackburn	5-2	4-1
Blackpool	3-1	3-1
Bolton	3-1	2-1
Burnley	4-4	2-4
Cardiff	3-2	2-3
Chelsea	4-2	3-2
Everton	2-0	3-1
Fulham	5-1	0-0
Leicester	2-3	2-1
Man City	1-1	1-0
Man United	4-1	0-2
Newcastle	1-2	4-3
Nottm Forest	1-0	4-0
Preston	5-0	1-0
Sheffield Wed	2-1	1-2
West Brom	1-2	3-1
West Ham Utd	2-0	3-0
Wolves	1-1	4-0

Final League Record

P	W	D	L	F	A	Pts	Pos
42	31	4	7	115	55	66	1st

FA Cup

Rnd 3	Charlton	(h)	3-2
Rnd 4	Crewe	(h)	5-1
Rnd 5	Aston Villa	(a)	2-0
Rnd 6	Sunderland	(a)	1-1
Replay	Sunderland	(h)	5-0
Semi-Final	Burnley	(n)	3-0
	Leicester	(W) (Wembley)	2-0

1961-2

Tottenham Hotspur had just won the First Division title and the FA Cup. How could they better that in 1961-2? The answer was simple — if the execution not easy — they now qualified for the European Cup. Could Spurs lift an incredible treble? In the end, they could not. But how close they came to the football feat to end all football feats.

In the First Division there was a new and unlikely force in the form of Ipswich Town. Spurs former England full-back Alf Ramsey — a man who played under that great thinker Arthur Rowe — proved himself a thinker when he devised a style of play which at first bemused opponents long enough to take the Suffolk club to the title in 1961-2. Withdrawing a winger into mid-field (actually, the 'winger' was wing-half Jimmy Leadbetter, wearing a number eleven shirt) Ramsey drew opposing defenders into the Ipswich half and then long balls from Leadbetter allowed the Ipswich strikers to reap the rewards.

> *In 1961-2 season ace scorer Jimmy Greaves joined Spurs from AC Milan for £99,999. Bill Nicholson did not want to sign the first £100,000 player. Greaves played in the FA Cup-winning team which was: Brown; Baker, Henry; Blanchflower, Norman, Mackay; Medwin, White, Smith, Greaves, Jones.*

Tottenham lost twice to Ipswich — 3-1 at White Hart Lane and 3-2 at Portman Road — and Ipswich finished top of the table, three points ahead of runners-up Burnley and four in front of Spurs, who came third with fourteen points fewer than the sixty-six which they won the title with the previous year. But they were in the running right until the final countdown and coupled with their successes in the FA and European Cups, it might well have been that 1961-2 proved an even more sensational season than the previous record-breaker. Certainly, for long periods there seemed nothing to stop Tottenham Hotspur's name going on all three trophies.

On 13 September 1961, Spurs played their first-ever European tie against Gornik Zabrze in the first-leg in Poland and were beaten 4-2. But the two goals scored by Jones and Dyson gave Tottenham hope for the return leg in London and on 20 September, Spurs gave one of their most epic performances. Wearing an all-white strip, Spurs demolished the Polish champions with a dazzling display under the White Hart Lane floodlights. Brilliant, controlled football saw the Poles ham-

mered 8-1. Cliff Jones scored a hat-trick and Bobby Smith hit two goals. Dyson, White and Blanchflower, from the penalty spot, added to the Gornik misery and Spurs had won 10-5 on aggregate. It seemed that Europe, like England, had no answer to Spurs ultimate mastery.

In November Feynoord, the Dutch champions, were also removed from the competition. Frank Saul (2) and Terry Dyson gave Spurs a 3-1 win in Rotterdam and at White Hart Lane, Dyson's goal made it 1-1 on the night and Spurs were safely through by a two-goal margin. A 1-0 first-leg defeat by Dukla Prague in Czechoslovakia was nothing to worry about. Spurs won 4-1 at home with Smith and Mackay each scoring twice and Tottenham were now in the semi-final of the European Cup at the first attempt. NO English club had so far won the trophy.

In the last four, Spurs faced the Eagles of Lisbon, Benfica, the Portuguese champions. The first-leg was played in Lisbon on 21 March and Spurs lost 3-1. Smith's goal gave Spurs everything to play for at White Hart Lane and even when Benfica extended their lead early on in the second-leg, Spurs got back in front 2-1 through Smith and a Blanchflower penalty and only a single goal stood between them and the levelling of the scores. That goal proved to be enough.

Bobby Smith restores the Tottenham lead against Burnley in the 1962 FA Cup Final.

Spurs abandoned the football which had gained them so much and in the cauldron-like atmosphere they pumped high, long balls about. They could not score again and although the game was an epic Euro-tie, it meant that Tottenham were out of the competition, having been unbeaten at home.

The FA Cup was the one trophy of the treble which Spurs did win. Although Bobby Smith missed games through injury, Frank Saul and Les Allen deputised ably, and Birmingham, Plymouth, West Brom and Aston Villa were all knocked out on the way to a semi-final at Hillsborough where Spurs beat Manchester United 3-1. Their Cup Final opponents were Burnley and Spurs beat them easily, 3-1. Jimmy Greaves kept up his record by scoring in his first-ever FA Cup Final and although Burnley equalised, Smith made it 2-1 before Blanchflower coolly put away a penalty to seal an interesting, but one-sided Final.

Danny Blanchflower's penalty kick puts the destination of the FA Cup beyond doubt.

First Division results 1961-2

	H	A
Arsenal	4-3	1-2
Aston Villa	1-0	0-0
Birmingham	3-1	3-2
Blackburn	4-1	1-0
Blackpool	5-2	2-1
Bolton	2-2	2-1
Burnley	4-2	2-2
Cardiff	3-2	1-1
Chelsea	5-2	2-0
Everton	3-1	0-3
Fulham	4-2	1-1
Ipswich	1-3	2-3
Leicester	1-2	3-2
Man City	2-0	2-6
Man Utd	2-2	0-1
Nottm Forest	4-2	0-2
Sheffield Utd	3-3	1-1
Sheffield Wed	4-0	0-0
West Brom	1-2	4-2
West Ham Utd	2-2	1-2
Wolves	1-0	1-3

Final League Record

P	W	D	L	F	A	Pts	Pos
42	21	10	11	88	69	52	3rd

FA Cup

Rnd 3	Birmingham	(a)	3-3
Replay	Birmingham	(h)	4-2
Rnd 4	Plymouth	(a)	5-1
Rnd 5	West Brom	(a)	4-2
Rnd 6	Aston Villa	(h)	2-0
Semi-final	Man United	(n)	3-1
Final	Burnley	(W) (Wembley)	3-1

European Cup

Pr Rnd (1st leg)	Gornik Zabrze	(a)	2-4
Pr Rnd (2nd leg)	Gornik Zabrze	(h)	8-1
1st Rnd (1st leg)	Feyenoord	(a)	3-1
1st Rnd (2nd leg)	Feyenoord	(h)	1-1
2nd Rnd (1st leg)	Dukla Prague	(a)	0-1
2nd Rnd (2nd leg)	Dukla Prague	(h)	4-1
Semi-final (1st leg)	Benfica	(a)	1-3
Semi-final (2nd leg)	Benfica	(h)	2-1

1962-3

The period from 1960 to 1963 was a truly great part of the Tottenham Hotspur story. League champions once, third place once, and then runners-up, coupled with successive FA Cup Final wins, the semi-finals of the European Cup, and then the winning of the Cup-winners Cup — the first British side to win a European trophy.

In the third season of that great run, Tottenham missed the First Division championship by six points with Everton winning the title. Yet Tottenham were in the running right up until the final stages and in finishing runners-up they proved themselves to be the most consistent First Division side of the early-Sixties. Again they scored over 100 goals in delighting crowds all over the country. Nottingham Forest felt the full blast of Spurs when they lost 9-2 at White Hart Lane and Liverpool (7-2), Manchester United (6-2) and Ipswich (5-0) were all left to lick their wounds as Tottenham rattled up another century of league goals.

In the FA Cup Spurs did not have things their own way, however, and the team which knocked them out at the first hurdle was Burnley, who had themselves been knocked out by Spurs on each of the previous two seasons — once in the semi-final and once in the Wembley Final itself. The White Hart Lane pitch was treacherous and icy when Burnley came to London and exacted revenge with a 3-0 win, the heat of which did not match the freezing temperature of the day. It was a bloody battle and resentment spilled over to make the game a most unedifying repeat of the previous season's Final. It was a disappointment but there was still the European Cup-winners Cup matches to look forward to and Spurs took full advantage of this by marching onwards to the final, despite losing the services of both Danny Blanchflower and Dave Mackay for part of the campaign — and Mackay's for the Final itself.

In the second round Tottenham were drawn to play Glasgow Rangers, the team which had become the first finalists of the Cup-winners Cup two seasons earlier. After their first round bye, Tottenham entertained Rangers at White Hart Lane and won 5-2. White, Greaves, Allen, Norman, and an own goal by a Scottish defender gave Spurs an invincible lead and in fact they also won 3-2 at Ibrox through two goals from Smith and one from Greaves. Straightaway, Spurs found themselves in the quarter-finals and although they had a temporary hiccup when Slovan Bratislava beat them 2-0 in Czechoslovakia, when the sides met at White Hart Lane there were goals for everyone as Tottenham romped home 6-0.

Greaves (2), Jones, White, Mackay and Smith all found themselves a place on the scoresheet.

The semi-final brought Tottenham up against the Yugoslavian Cup-holders OFK Belgrade and on 24 April 1963 Spurs won 2-1 in Belgrade. John White and Terry Dyson scored for Spurs and when the return leg was played on 1 May, Spurs increased their lead to an overall 5-2 when Mackay, Jones and Smith added the finishing touches to an immaculate Tottenham display which had taken them one stage further than their European Cup quest of twelve months earlier.

> *The Spurs team which won the European Cup-winners Cup in Rotterdam was: Brown; Baker, Henry; Blanchflower, Norman, Marchi, Jones, White, Smith, Greaves, Dyson.*

The European Cup-winners Cup Final was held in Rotterdam on 15 May 1963 and Tottenham Hotspur became the first British club to win a European trophy when they beat the Spanish giants, Atletico Madrid with a superb display of football that finally enabled them to complete the task by an incredible 5-1 scoreline. Spurs led 2-0 at half-time and although Collar pulled a penalty back for the Spaniards, Tottenham sealed their win. The goals came from Greaves (2), Dyson (2) and White.

Greaves had scored thirty-seven goals in the league and cups and he was chosen as Footballer of the Year by the game's commentators. Spurs left for a close season tour to South Africa and after 108 competitive games in two seasons, the players looked forward to a well-earned rest.

First Division 1962-3

	H	A
Arsenal	4-4	3-2
Aston Villa	4-2	1-2
Birmingham	3-0	2-0
Blackburn...................	4-1	0-3
Blackpool	2-0	2-1
Bolton	4-1	0-1
Burnley	1-1	1-2
Everton	0-0	0-1
Fulham	1-1	2-0
Ipswich	5-0	4-2
Leicester	4-0	2-2
Leyton O	2-0	5-1
Liverpool	7-2	2-5
Man City	4-2	0-1
Man United	6-2	2-0
Nottm Forest	9-2	1-1
Sheffield Utd	4-2	1-3
Sheffield Wed..............	1-1	1-3
West Brom	2-1	2-1
West Ham	4-4	6-1
Wolves	1-2	2-2

Final League Record

P	W	D	L	F	A	Pts	Pos
42	23	9	10	111	62	55	2nd

FA Cup

Rnd 3	Burnley	(h)	0-3

Cup-winners' Cup

Rnd 2 (1st leg)	Rangers	(h)	5-2
Rnd 2 (2nd leg)	Rangers	(a)	3-2
Rnd 3 (1st leg)	Slovan B	(a)	0-2
Rnd 3 (2nd leg)	Slovan B	(h)	6-0
Semi-final (1st leg)	OFK Belgrade	(a)	2-1
Semi-final (2nd leg)	OFK Belgrade	(h)	3-1
Final	Atletico Madrid	(n)	5-1

Danny Blanchflower guided Spurs to the European Cup-winners Cup final – and they became the first English club to win a European trophy.

Terry Dyson fails to beat Blackburn Rovers goalkeeper Fred Else in the League match at White Hart Lane in September 1962. But Spurs eventually won 4-1.

1963-4

Tottenham Hotspur's troubles began when Terry Medwin broke a leg on the close season tour to South Africa, and ill-luck was to dog Spurs throughout the 1963-4 season. The magnificent Tottenham team of the previous three seasons was showing signs of wear. In the First Division programme there was an ominous sign when Tottenham went to Ewood Park, Blackburn in the first few weeks of the season and were crushed 7-2 — their heaviest defeat since Newcastle beat them twelve years before, when their team was about to undergo a similar demise. Manchester United then won 4-1 at Old Trafford and Spurs fans sensed that they had seen it all before.

In December, Spurs met United again, this time in the second round of the European Cup-winners Cup. Tottenham were in the competition again as winners, United because they held the FA Cup. On 3 December, at White Hart Lane, Mackay and Dyson gave Spurs a 2-0 win. It was not a particularly big lead to take to Old Trafford but it was still a lead. Seven days later in Manchester, Tottenham suffered their second big blow of the season. United were leading 3-1 but the Jimmy Greaves goal meant that the scores were still level on aggregate. Then disaster struck. Dave Mackay broke his leg and Tottenham — as well as losing the indomitable Mackay for heaven knows how long — were down to ten men because there were no substitutes allowed in those days. Yet still they held on and it was not until Bobby Charlton scored United's fourth that Tottenham were finally out by the slender margin of one goal, despite the severe blow they had suffered.

In the third round of the FA Cup, Spurs drew 1-1 with Chelsea and lost the replay at Stamford Bridge 2-0. Suddenly, there was only the league to interest the fans at White Hart Lane and although Spurs were always around the edge of the title race, it was Manchester United and Liverpool who were looking most likely to lift the championship.

But 1963-4 will be remembered most of all for the awful, tragic accident which put even the breaking of Dave Mackay's leg out of everyone's mind. John White, the ghostly legend of Tottenham Hotspur, was sheltering under a tree during a thunderstorm when the tree was struck by lightning — a million-to-one chance — and White was killed. Football was stunned. At the age of twenty-six, White had achieved so much. And yet there was so much more left for him to achieve. Already, White had captured the hearts and minds of millions of soccer fans with a grace and poise found only in the greatest of great sportsmen. It was this utter gracefulness which made White the truly world-class performer which he was. He would float effortlessly about the field. In one cruel flash of lightning, his life and that grace were extinguished for ever.

The top of the First Division in 1963-4 finally ended like this:						
	P	W	D	L	F	A	Pts
Liverpool	42	26	5	11	92	45	57
Man United	42	23	7	12	90	62	53
Everton	42	21	10	11	84	64	52
Tottenham	42	22	7	13	97	81	51
Chelsea	42	20	10	12	72	56	50

During the season, Danny Blanchflower played his last game for Tottenham Hotspur before retiring. In all his appearances in the First Division totalled fifteen that fateful season. A new star in the guise of Alan Mullery came into the Spurs team. But the names of White and Blanchflower had gone out of it for ever.

Everton's Tony Kay clears from John White as the Merseysiders win 4-2 at White Hart Lane in March 1964.

John White was tragically killed while sheltering from a thunderstorm.

Even in the most fortunate of circumstances it would have taken Spurs time to recover from the fact that players were missing for most of the season. In the tragic times of 1963-4, Spurs did creditably well to finish as high as fourth place in the First Division to maintain a record of being in the top four for five consecutive seasons. In addition, Jimmy Greaves scored thirty-five more goals to bring his career record past the 200 mark — the youngest player ever to reach the milestone. But these facts and figures were the tail-end of another golden Tottenham era. Just as before, there were occasional flashes of that old brilliance throughout the season (ask Blackpool, Birmingham and Ipswich, who all had six goals put past them at White Hart Lane). But another Spurs dynasty had died.

First Division results 1963-4

	H	A
Arsenal	3-1	4-4
Aston Villa	3-1	4-2
Birmingham	6-1	2-1
Blackburn	4-1	2-7
Blackpool	6-1	2-0
Bolton	1-0	3-1
Burnley	3-2	2-7
Chelsea	1-2	3-0
Everton	2-4	0-1
Fulham	1-0	1-1
Ipswich	6-3	3-2
Leicester	1-1	1-0
Liverpool	1-3	1-3
Man United	2-3	1-4
Nottm Forest	4-1	2-1
Sheffield Utd	0-0	3-3
Sheffield Wed	1-1	0-2
Stoke	2-1	1-2
West Brom	0-2	4-4
West Ham	3-0	0-4
Wolves	4-3	4-1

Final League Record

P	W	D	L	F	A	Pts	Pos
42	22	7	13	97	81	51	4th

FA Cup

Rnd 3	Chelsea	(h)	1-1
Replay	Chelsea	(a)	0-2

Cup-winners' Cup

Rnd 2 (1st leg)	Man United	(h)	2-0
Rnd 2 (2nd leg)	Man United	(a)	1-4

1964-5

To look at the record books for season 1964-5 is to wonder if Tottenham Hotspur played with two different sides throughout the campaign! On the one hand, Spurs home record suggests that the team would surpass even the legendary feats of the 'double' winning side of 1960-1. On the other, Tottenham's record on opponent's grounds suggests that Spurs would be relegated, many points adrift of the rest of the stragglers.

First, the White Hart Lane record: throughout 1964-5, Tottenham were the only club in the First Division to keep their home record intact. Twenty-one games brought Spurs thirty-nine of their eventual forty-five points! They won eighteen matches and drew three, scoring sixty-five goals and conceding only twenty. Only Chelsea, Everton and Leeds came away from Tottenham with a point. The rest perished along the way, with Wolves (who lost 7-4), Leicester (6-2) and Blackburn (5-2) enduring the best of Spurs' immaculate home form.

Away from White Hart Lane, Tottenham could do nothing right. In their twenty-one away games, they managed only one victory—a 2-1 win at Nottingham Forest's City Ground on the banks of the River Trent—and just four were drawn, those matches at Blackpool, Burnley, Liverpool and Sheffield United. Spurs could manage only twenty-two goals for, while in losing sixteen away games, they conceded fifty-one. Amazingly, Spurs managed to finish sixth in the First Division in spite of (or perhaps, thanks to) this bizarre Jekyll and Hyde record. Spurs conceded nearly twice as many goals as champions Manchester United—but scored only two less.

Despite their appalling away record, Spurs finished quite well-placed in the First Division of 1964-5. The top placings were:

	P	W	D	L	F	A	Pts
Man United	*42*	*26*	*9*	*7*	*89*	*39*	*61*
Leeds Utd	*42*	*26*	*9*	*7*	*83*	*52*	*61*
Chelsea	*42*	*24*	*8*	*10*	*89*	*54*	*46*
Everton	*42*	*17*	*15*	*10*	*69*	*60*	*49*
Nottm Forest	*42*	*17*	*13*	*12*	*71*	*67*	*47*
Tottenham	*42*	*19*	*7*	*16*	*87*	*71*	*45*
Liverpool	*42*	*17*	*10*	*15*	*67*	*73*	*44*

Considering this appalling away record, only the champions were watched by more people away from home. No less than 721,213 fans (averaging over 34,000 a game) packed in to see this Tottenham side which could not do a thing right away from home. With a White Hart Lane aggregate of 827,213 (well over 39,000 per game), Spurs pulled in a total of over one-and-a-half million fans in 1964-5. Even Chelsea, who finished three places above Spurs could not match that and it is still a measure of how magical is the name of Tottenham Hotspur —win, lose or draw they are still one of the most famous football clubs in the world.

In the FA Cup, Tottenham Hotspur's record away from home was just as bad; their White Hart Lane figures just as good. In the first stage of their journey to Wembley, Tottenham had to travel to the West Country where Third Division (South) Torquay United held them to a 3-3 draw at Plainmoor. In the London replay, Spurs had no inhibitions and wiped out the Devon challenge as easily as the 5-1 scoreline suggests. In the next round Ipswich Town came to White Hart Lane and Spurs walloped the Suffolk side 5-0 to meet Chelsea at

Dave Mackay recovers from his second broken leg in ten months to join Terry Medwin for a White Hart Lane training session. It was Christmas 1964 when doctors told Mackay that he would play again.

Spurs 1964-5 line-up. For the third successive season Jimmy Greaves (third from right, front row) had carried Tottenham's attack and finished leading scorer again with twenty-nine League goals.

Stamford Bridge in the sixth round. The way Spurs were playing, a home draw in every round would have at least seen them to the semi-finals. But at Chelsea they continued their abysmal form and lost by the only goal of the game.

The season finished with Jimmy Greaves again the Tottenham leading scorer with twenty-nine league goals. For the third successive season, the cheerful little Londoner had carried much of the Spurs attack on his own not-so-broad shoulders, nipping in to convert half-chances into precious goals.

The changing personnel continued apace. Faces which left the Tottenham ground were Les Allen, Tony Marchi, Peter Baker, Terry Dyson and Terry Medwin. Medwin was forced to retire following the broken leg he had suffered in South Africa. Dave Mackay was set for a return the following season after breaking his leg for a second time; and during the 1964-5 season Alan Gilzean joined the club from Dundee, while young Joe Kinnear signed full-time professional forms. It had been a funny season — in the peculiar, not amusing sense — and there was to be some more rebuilding yet. But another Spurs side was emerging which would take honours back to White Hart Lane. The Tottenham cock would crow again.

First Division results 1964-5

	H	A
Arsenal	3-1	1-3
Aston Villa	4-0	0-1
Birmingham	4-1	0-1
Blackburn	5-2	1-3
Blackpool	4-1	1-1
Burnley	4-1	2-2
Chelsea	1-1	1-3
Everton	2-2	1-4
Fulham	3-0	1-4
Leeds	0-0	1-3
Leicester	6-2	2-4
Liverpool	3-0	1-1
Man United	1-0	1-4
Nottm Forest	4-0	2-1
Sheffield Utd	2-0	3-3
Sheffield Wed..............	3-2	0-1
Stoke	2-1	0-2
Sunderland	3-0	1-2
West Brom	1-0	0-2
West Ham Utd	3-2	2-3
Wolves	7-4	1-3

Final League Record

P	W	D	L	F	A	Pts	Pos
42	19	7	16	87	71	45	6th

FA Cup

Rnd 3	Torquay Utd	(a)	3-3
Replay	Torquay Utd	(h)	5-1
Rnd 4	Ipswich	(h)	5-0
Rnd 5	Chelsea	(a)	0-1

1965-6

From a strictly playing point of view, season 1965-6 had little to contribute towards the story of Tottenham Hotspur Football Club. The team finished eighth in the First Division and reached the fifth round of the FA Cup before being knocked out at Preston North End. But there were other milestones, both within the club and outside of, but still affecting it. Tottenham's manager, Bill Nicholson completed thirty years service with the club he had joined in the years leading up to World War II. As a player, coach and finally manager, Nicholson had seen most of the glory which had come Spurs way in the last three decades. He had himself won an England cap, a First Division title medal, and as a manager had steered the club to the 'double' and to

European honours. To mark his years of dedicated service to Spurs, the Tottenham chairman Frederick Wale presented Nicholson with a silver rosebowl.

1965-6 was also the season that the Football League finally agreed to the use of substitutes, although by confining their use for that first season to the replacement of players lost through injury, the League only opened the system to allegations of abuse. Later, when they agreed that any player, apart from one who had been sent off, could be replaced, the whole system had a much healthier ring to it. But like so many other clubs, Spurs had suffered when reduced to ten men and they were as pleased as any team to see that football would, in future, be contested between teams of equal numbers.

Finally, that summer saw England take the World Cup for the first, and so far only, time by beating West Germany 4-2 at Wembley. Individual club glory belonged to Spurs neighbours West Ham United who supplied England with three players, including the captain and also the man who scored a historic hat-trick in the Final. Bobby Moore, Geoff Hurst and Martin Peters stole the thunder while Spurs Jimmy Greaves was left out of the final England team by another ex-Spur, Alf Ramsey, now manager of the national side.

When Maurice Norman broke his leg in November 1965 he joined an unfortunate, but select, band of Tottenham players who had done the same. They included Fred Channell, George Greenfield, Willie Evans, Cliff Jones, Terry Medwin and Dave Mackay . . . twice. Sadly, Norman, like Channell, never played top-class football again.

In the First Division, Tottenham's invincible home record had gone to the extent of conceding thirty-seven goals at White Hart Lane, a home figure only one goal better than bottom club Blackburn Rovers, and five goals more than the other relegated club Northampton Town had conceded at their own County Ground. Equally, Spurs found it difficult to score away from home and only twenty goals were netted away from White Hart Lane. The reasons for this Tottenham failure were manifold but not least of them was the fact that Spurs had lost several key players at vital times during the season.

Bill Nicholson completed thirty years service at White Hart Lane.

Jimmy Greaves, Bill Brown, Cliff Jones and Maurice Norman had all been laid-up for quite long spells. In fact Norman, who had broken his leg in a friendly against a Hungarian XI during November, was never to play in the Tottenham Hotspur first team again. His injury was so severe as to render him unfit for top-class soccer.

Spurs always seem to figure in those entries in the record books that cover high-scoring matches and 1965-6 was no exception. When Aston Villa came to White Hart Lane for the First Division fixture, the sides shared ten goals equally to give a score-draw with the most unlikely result of 5-5. After beating Middlesbrough and Burnley at White Hart Lane in the third and fourth rounds of the FA Cup, Tottenham journeyed up to Lancashire and Preston's Deepdale, where they were beaten 2-1. Yet that Cup defeat signalled the last time that Spurs would lose an FA Cup-tie for almost two years. Bill Nicholson's Tottenham Hotspur Mark Two was nearly ready to take off.

First Division results 1965-6

	H	A
Arsenal	2-2	1-1
Aston Villa	5-5	2-3
Blackburn.	4-0	1-0
Blackpool	4-0	0-0
Burnley	0-1	1-1
Chelsea	4-2	1-2
Everton	2-2	1-3
Fulham	4-3	2-0
Leeds	3-2	0-2
Leicester	4-2	2-2
Liverpool	2-1	0-1
Man United	5-1	1-5
Newcastle	2-2	0-0
Northampton	1-1	2-0
Nottm Forest	2-3	0-1
Sheffield Utd	1-0	3-1
Sheffield Wed.	2-3	1-1
Stoke	2-2	1-0
Sunderland.	3-0	0-2
West Brom	2-1	1-2
West Ham	1-4	0-2

Final League Record

P	W	D	L	F	A	Pts	Pos
42	16	12	14	75	66	44	8th

FA Cup

Rnd 3	Middlesbrough	(h)	4-0
Rnd 4	Burnley	(h)	4-3
Rnd 5	Preston	(a)	1-2

Jimmy Greaves missed much of the season through injury.

1966-7

We have said before that Tottenham Hotspur have sometimes had a bit of Jekyll and Hyde about them. The 1966-7 season was no exception, except that this time, Spurs inconsistencies were not separated home and away, or confined to occasional flashes of brilliance. This time their season was split into two separate halves. Indeed, it has been said that if the season had started in January, Spurs would have lifted the 'double' again!

The season opened with new faces. Terry Venables was signed from Chelsea and big Mike England, the Welsh international centre-half, came from Blackburn to replace Maurice Norman. In addition, Pat Jennings began where he had left off the previous season. The Irish goalkeeper signed from Watford in 1964, took his chance with both hands when Bill Brown was injured.

After a good start — home wins over Leeds and Arsenal and an away 2-0 victory over Newcastle United at St James's Park — augered well for the immediate future. But Spurs were not able to maintain that early impetus and although Kinnear and

Robertson (not pictured) scores Spurs first goal in the 1967 FA Cup Final against Chelsea.

Frank Saul (no 11) scores Spurs second goal and Chelsea are beaten.

Beal were now holding down the full-back positions with some sterling displays in front of the increasingly-safe Jennings, and even when Mike England was safe and sure at centre-half, there were other areas of the Tottenham side where concern was showing. A classic example was little Cliff Jones. The Welsh international had taken some fearful punishment over the years — broken leg and all — and he was showing signs that the grit and endeavour was understandably being knocked out of him. But Jones's problems were only part of a general lack of form which cost Spurs the First Division title. In a one-month period over October-November, they lost three successive home games and took one point from three away games. One point from twelve is the sort of form from which no team can fully recover in a season.

After ignoring the Football League Cup for the first few years of its infancy, Spurs decided to try it for size and were immediately beaten 1-0 at West Ham United in the second round. So the bad run continued. Over Christmas 1966, Spurs lost three points to West Brom — drawing 0-0 at home and going down 3-0 at the Hawthorns — and by the turn of the year, Spurs were in trouble.

Then, inexplicably, it all changed for the better. From the first Saturday in 1967, Spurs went twenty-four matches without once tasting defeat. It was a run too late to give them the First Division title. But it was good enough to take them to third place in the table and into the FA Cup Final where they created a new record. In the third round of the Cup, Spurs drew 0-0 at The Den and Alan Gilzean scored the only goal of the replay to knock out Millwall. Then Gilzean (2) and Greaves beat Portsmouth 3-1 at home, and then Greaves scored both goals against Bristol City in Spurs 2-0 win also at at White Hart Lane, although City missed a twice-taken penalty.

In the sixth round Birmingham held Spurs 0-0 at St Andrews and could do nothing in the replay

> *Spurs not only became only the second club to win all five FA Cup Finals in which they played. They are the only club still in existence to do so. The years are: 1901, 1921, 1961, 1962, 1967. The 1967 side was: Jennings; Kinnear, Knowles; Mullery, England, Mackay; Robertson, Greaves, Gilzean, Venables, Saul. The attendance was 100,000 and the receipts £109,649.*

Spurs 1966-7 team which took the FA Cup and finished third in the First Division.

when Greaves (2), Venables (2), Gilzean and Saul saw them off, 6-0 into the semi-final. There they met Nottingham Forest at Hillsborough. Forest were on target for the 'double' but Greaves and Saul kept that particular record in Tottenham's court and Forest went down 2-1. They also missed the First Division title by four points to finish runners-up.

And so to Wembley and an all-London FA Cup Final against Chelsea. Spurs won 2-1 but they were more in command than the score suggests. Mike England dominated the much-travelled Tony Hateley and at the interval Spurs were a goal ahead when Jimmy Robertson volleyed home after Ron Harris had blocked Mullery's shot. In the second-half, Saul made it 2-0 and although Bobby Tambling pulled a goal back for Chelsea, Tottenham held on to become the second club in history to play in five FA Cup Finals and win the lot.

First Division results 1966-7

	H	A
Arsenal	3-1	2-0
Aston Villa	0-1	3-3
Blackpool	1-3	2-2
Burnley	2-0	2-2
Chelsea	1-1	0-3
Everton	2-0	1-0
Fulham	4-2	4-3
Leeds	3-1	2-3
Leicester	2-0	1-0
Liverpool	2-1	0-0
Man City	1-1	2-1
Man United	2-1	0-1
Newcastle	4-0	2-0
Nottm Forest	2-1	1-1
Sheffield Utd	2-0	1-2
Sheffield Wed	2-1	0-1
Southampton	5-3	1-0
Stoke	2-0	0-2
Sunderland	1-0	1-0
West Brom	0-0	0-3
West Ham Utd	3-4	2-0

Final League Record

P	W	D	L	F	A	Pts	Pos
42	24	8	10	71	48	56	3rd

FA Cup

Rnd 3	Millwall	(a)	0-0
Replay	Millwall	(h)	1-0
Rnd 4	Portsmouth	(h)	3-1
Rnd 5	Bristol City	(h)	2-0
Rnd 6	Birmingham	(a)	0-0
Replay	Birmingham	(h)	6-0
Semi-final	Nottm Forest	(n)	2-1
Final	Chelsea	(W) (Wembley)	2-1

Football League Cup

Rnd 2	West Ham Utd	(a)	0-1

1967-8

Spurs fans had another season of European competition to look forward to as a result of the FA Cup Final win which put Tottenham Hotspur in the European Cup-winners Cup for 1967-8. Of the famous 'double' team of 1960-1, only Dave Mackay remained, while Jimmy Greaves was in the side which won the Cup-winners Cup in 1963.

Spurs first hurdle in an attempt to recover the Cup was against Hajduk Split. On 20 September 1967, Tottenham won 2-0 in Yugoslavia, thanks to goals from the two Jimmies—Robertson and Greaves. Robertson (2), Gilzean and Venables scored when the Split team came to White Hart Lane for the return leg and Spurs went into the next round, though not before Hajduk had scored three goals themselves to bring the final aggregate to 6-3.

The second round first-leg match against the French Cup-holders Lyon in France is perhaps best forgotten. Lyon won 1-0 but in holding them to a single goal, Spurs lost Alan Mullery, sent off with Lyon's Andre Guy after an ugly incident. Spurs won the second-leg all right, but they went out of the competition. Although Greaves (2), Jones and Gilzean scored four for Spurs, Rambert, Di Nallo and Bouffa hit three for Lyon and with the aggregate scores level, the Frenchmen's away goals counted double. Spurs had been dumped out by the unfancied French side and could now rue the fact

Jimmy Robertson who scored three goals in Spurs two European Cup-winners Cup ties with Yugoslavian Cup winners Hajduk Split.

that they had not scored a goal in Lyon. Yet still Tottenham had an unbeaten record in European competitions on their own ground. It was not enough to give them a second bite of the European cherry.

Tottenham Hotspur obviously needed extra goal power and Nicholson saw it in Southampton's big striker, Martin Chivers. Spurs manager went to The Dell and paid the Saints a record £125,000 for Chivers. It was a far cry from those days in the early part of the century when Spurs had attracted a record crowd to Southampton after the notorious affair of 'Payne's boots', when the hint that Spurs were actually *paying* players was enough to send shudders round southern football. Chivers arrived at Tottenham in January and although he added a much-needed punch to the Spurs forward line it would be some while before Tottenham fans would see him at his absolute best. The team was not playing well and even the arrival of the Southampton player would not herald an immediate change in Spurs fortunes.

Yet still Tottenham managed their usual handful of big scores. Even in the most mediocre of seasons clubs had always a fear that they would run into a Spurs side bang on form. In 1967-8 it was the turn of Southampton to have six goals rammed past them at White Hart Lane while Burnley and West Ham United each lost by conceding five goals against Tottenham at their rampant best. But the First Division was always running away from Spurs and they did well to finish as high as seventh, while the title went to Manchester again, although this time it was City who took it. But for Spurs seventh was a failure; it was four places lower than the previous year and by White Hart Lane standards, not a good year.

> *Dave Mackay, who left Spurs at the end of the 1967-8 season, always seemed a giant on the field. In fact the barrel-chested Scotsman stood only 5ft 8in. At times, though, he seemed ten feel tall!*

Again, when league matches were not going well, Spurs fans looked to the FA Cup for some success and for a while their prayers looked like being answered. In the third round Spurs did well to draw 2-2 at Old Trafford in a thrilling tie. The replay was a shambles. Joe Kinnear and Brian Kidd were both sent off and from Spurs point of view, the only redeeming feature was that Jimmy Robertson scored the only goal of the game in extra time.

Preston were hustled out 3-1 at home and then Spurs faced Liverpool in the fifth round. A 1-1 draw at White Hart Lane meant that Tottenham had to go to Anfield where they had not won for over fifty years. This was to prove no exception and the Reds won 2-1 with an ease that is belied by the narrow scoreline. And that was how Spurs season ended. There was nothing more to play for. The team was safe and yet it could not win the title. The saddest part of 1967-8 was the last appearance of that old war horse, Dave Mackay. Brian Clough was taking him to Derby to add a new dimension to the Scotsman's already distinguished career.

First Division results 1967-8

	H	A
Arsenal	1-0	0-4
Burnley	5-0	1-5
Chelsea	2-0	0-2
Coventry	4-2	3-2
Everton	1-1	1-0
Fulham	2-2	2-1
Leeds	2-1	0-1
Leicester	0-1	3-2
Liverpool	1-1	1-1
Man City	1-3	1-4
Man United	1-2	1-3
Newcastle	1-1	3-1
Nottm Forest	1-1	0-0
Sheffield Utd	1-1	2-3
Sheffield Wed	2-1	2-1
Southampton	6-1	2-1
Stoke	3-0	1-2
Sunderland	3-0	1-0
West Brom	0-0	0-2
West Ham Utd	5-1	1-2
Wolves	2-1	1-2

Final League Record

P	W	D	L	F	A	Pts	Pos
42	19	9	14	70	59	47	7th

Terry Venables also played his part in removing Hajduk Split. Venables' goal in the second leg at White Hart Lane helped Spurs to win 6-3 on aggregate.

FA Cup

Rnd 3	Man United	(a)	2-2
Replay	Man United	(h)	1-0
Rnd 4	Preston	(h)	3-1
Rnd 5	Liverpool	(h)	1-1
Replay	Liverpool	(a)	1-2

Cup-winners' Cup

Rnd 1 (1st leg)	Hajduk Split	(a)	2-0
Rnd 1 (2nd leg)	Hajduk Split	(h)	4-3
Rnd 2 (1st leg)	Lyon	(a)	0-1
Rnd 2 (2nd leg)	Lyon	(h)	4-3

Spurs lost on away-goals rule

1968-9

Another frustrating season for Tottenham Hotspur Football Club. Spurs finished sixth in the First Division and got to the quarter-finals of the FA Cup and the semi-finals of the Football League Cup. But again, they ended up with nothing to show for their efforts in three highly-competitive trophies.

Throughout the season there were team changes, enforced either by injury or by the fact that some players had no longer anything to offer Tottenham Hotspur. It was particularly sad to see Cliff Jones depart for Fulham. The Welsh winger had signed for Spurs in 1958 and had given the club tremendous service for a decade or more. Jones was the last of the old Spurs team and his departure signalled the breaking of the last link with a distinguished part of the Tottenham tale. Jimmy Robertson was also on the move—to Arsenal—while David Jenkins travelled in the opposite direction and joined Spurs from Highbury. In February, one of QPR's brilliant Morgan twins — Roger — was signed by Spurs. At the end of the season, Terry Venables left White Hart Lane for Loftus Road and the blue and white hoops of Rangers. Venables had been used in midfield and he never looked really at home since joining Spurs from Chelsea where his tremendous shooting power made him a striker to be feared.

One blow which Spurs could well have done without was the injury to Martin Chivers. In the 2-1 win over Nottingham Forest in September, Chivers was showing all his skill and power and Nicholson must have felt particularly excited as his signing chose that game to show all his potential. Then he was injured and his ligaments proved so badly damaged that an operation was necessry. Spurs had lost a striker at the precise time that he was 'coming good'.

Yet Jimmy Greaves was still scoring goals to lift the crowd. A hat-trick at Tottenham in the 3-2 win over Leicester City in October continued a truly brilliant goal. The little Londoner weaved his way round five Leicester defenders before planting the ball past the emergent Peter Shilton. England's future goalkeeper could only watch the ball sail into his net.

In November Greaves scored Spurs goal in the 1-1 draw with Stoke City to become the first player in the club's history to score 200 league goals for them. Once he stood complaining about the Liverpool wall not being back ten yards while he waited to take a free-kick. The referee signalled for the kick to be taken but still Greaves stood on the ball, pointing, while Lawrence dashed about his goal line. With the Liverpool defenders off guard for that split second, Greaves flashed the ball home. It was the mark of a genius.

Three West Midlands clubs — Walsall, Wolves and Aston Villa — were removed from the FA Cup

before Spurs went out in the sixth round, beaten 1-0 by the eventual Cup winners, Manchester City at Maine Road.

In only their second attempt at the Football League Cup Tottenham reached the semi-finals. The road to the last four was varied. There were wins over Aston Villa, Exeter City, Peterborough United and Southampton before Spurs met Arsenal in a two-legged semi-final. At Highbury in the first-leg in November, John Radford scored the only goal of the game; it was Radford who, in effect, scored the winner at White Hart Lane a fortnight later. Jimmy Greaves equalised the aggregate, Radford made it 1-1 on the night, 2-1 on aggregate, and Spurs season was to empty once again.

The second leg of the Spurs-Arsenal Football League Cup semi-final at White Hart Lane in November 1968 was marred by some nasty incidents early in the game. Some of the 'needle' often associated with local Derby games spoiled what could have been an excellent game.

▲

Jimmy Robertson in action in the 3-2 win over Leicester at White Hart Lane. Robertson was soon on the move to Spurs North London rivals, Arsenal.

Spurs 'nearly' team of 1968-9 – sixth in the First Division, quarter-finalists in the FA Cup and semi-finalists in the League Cup. Martin Chivers (third from left, front row) ◄ missed much of the action through ligament trouble.

First Division results 1968-9

	H	A
Arsenal	1-2	0-1
Burnley	7-0	2-2
Chelsea	1-0	2-2
Coventry	2-0	2-1
Everton	1-1	2-0
Ipswich	2-2	1-0
Leeds	0-0	0-0
Leicester	3-2	0-1
Liverpool	2-1	0-1
Man City	1-1	0-4
Man United	2-2	1-3
Newcastle	0-1	2-2
Nottm Forest	2-1	2-0
QPR	3-2	1-1
Sheffield Wed	1-2	0-0
Southampton	2-1	1-2
Stoke	1-1	1-1
Sunderland	5-1	0-0
West Brom	1-1	3-4
West Ham Utd	1-0	2-2
Wolves	1-1	0-2

Final League Record

P	W	D	L	F	A	Pts	Pos
42	14	17	11	61	51	45	6th

FA Cup

Rnd 3	Walsall	(a)	1-0
Rnd 4	Wolves	(h)	2-1
Rnd 5	Aston Villa	(h)	3-2
Rnd 6	Man City	(a)	0-1

Football League Cup

Rnd 2	Aston Villa	(a)	4-1
Rnd 3	Exeter City	(h)	6-3
Rnd 4	Peterborough	(h)	1-0
Rnd 5	Southampton	(h)	1-0
Semi-final	Arsenal (1st leg)	(a)	0-1
Semi-final	Arsenal (2nd leg)	(h)	1-1

1969-70

To finish in the top eleven of the Football League's First Division every season for over ten years is surely a record of model consistency. If you add to that all the honours which came to White Hart Lane during that period then it can be seen that Bill Nicholson's influence on the club was even greater as a manager than it had been as a player. And yet people talk of the Tottenham 'lean years' when they talk of the late Sixties. The 1969-70 season was a 'lean' year by Tottenham standards when they finished eleventh in the First Division and were knocked out of both the FA and Football League Cups in the early stages. Yet the operative phrase is 'by Tottenham's own standards' because there is no doubt that many clubs would have happily settled for what Spurs achieved.

There were, however, some low spots. Like the FA Cup fourth round exit at the hands of Crystal Palace. Spurs had already had trouble in removing Bradford City from the third round, drawing 2-2 in Bradford before beating the lowly Yorkshire side 5-0 at White Hart Lane. Then Palace held Spurs to a goalless draw before winning 1-0 at Selhurst Park. By the same scoreline, Wolves had knocked Spurs out of the Football League Cup.

In the First Division Tottenham fans had the one consolation that their team had beaten Arsenal twice during 1969-70. At Highbury on an evening in September, Martin Chivers, Alan Gilzean and John Pratt earned them a 3-2 win; and on the very last day of the season, Gilzean it was who scored the lone goal when the two old North London rivals met at White Hart Lane to conclude their programmes.

But there were some silly defeats at home, notably against Everton, Wolves, Sunderland and Coventry, while Manchester City won handsomely by 3-0 at White Hart Lane. Early in the season Spurs went to Derby where Dave Mackay had returned to First Division football with the newly-promoted Rams. Over 40,000 people broke Derby's Baseball Ground record to see Spurs humbled 5-0. Mackay admitted afterwards to being both elated and sad. It must have been a difficult experience for the old Spur.

Spurs had mixed fortunes so far as the unofficial London 'championship' went. Chelsea rode high in third place while Arsenal were a place below Tottenham, while West Ham and more so, Crystal Palace, fought their way clear of relegation, Palace finishing just a point ahead of Sunderland. But there was hope on the horizon for Spurs. During 1969-70, the Tottenham Hotspur reserve side finished runners-up to Arsenal in the Football Combination and were also semi-finalists in the

Jimmy Greaves bursts through the Manchester City defence during the First Division game at White Hart Lane in September 1969. But City won 3-0.

First Division results 1969-70

	H	A
Arsenal	1-0	3-2
Burnley	4-0	2-0
Chelsea	1-1	0-1
Coventry	1-2	2-3
Crystal Palace	2-0	2-0
Derby	2-1	0-5
Everton	0-1	2-3
Ipswich	3-2	0-2
Leeds	1-1	1-3
Liverpool	0-2	0-0
Man City	0-3	1-1
Man United	2-1	1-3
Newcastle	2-1	2-1
Nottm Forest	4-1	2-2
Sheffield Wed	1-0	1-0
Southampton	0-1	2-2
Stoke	1-0	1-1
Sunderland	0-1	1-2
West Brom	2-0	1-1
West Ham	0-2	1-0
Wolves	0-1	2-2

Final League Record

P	W	D	L	F	A	Pts	Pos
42	17	9	16	54	55	43	11th

FA Cup

Rnd 3	Bradford C	(a)	2-2
Replay	Bradford C	(h)	5-0
Rnd 4	C Palace	(h)	0-0
Replay	C Palace	(a)	0-1

Football League Cup

Rnd 2	Wolves	(a)	0-1

Combination Cup, while Pat Welton's youth side brought the FA Youth Cup to Tottenham for the first time.

Tottenham's youngsters beat West Ham United 6-1 in the first round; Leyton Orient 2-0 in the second; Arsenal 1-0 in the third; Reading 2-0 in the fourth; and reached the final by beating Stoke City 2-0 in the semi-final to earn themselves a game against Coventry City.

> *The Spurs team which won the FA Youth Cup contained some names that would become famous in the next ten years: It was: Daines; Almond, Jones; Dillon, Edwards, Souness; Oliver, Turner, Clarke, Perryman, Flanagan.*

In the first leg of the Final, Spurs won 1-0 but Coventry reversed that scoreline in the return leg and the Final went to a third match which ended 2-2. Eventually, Graeme Souness, who went to the same school as Dave Mackay, broke the deadlock and scored the only goal of the game on Millwall's Den to give Spurs the FA Youth Cup after a Final which had run to four matches. The future looked bright for a Spurs team which had lost Greaves, Gilzean, Kinnear and Knowles, all dropped after the Palace FA Cup defeat. With Martin Peters arriving from West Ham for a record £200,000, Nicholson was looking to his youngsters for success in the Seventies.

Crystal Palace goalkeeper John Jackson and defender Roger Hynd combine to thwart Alan Gilzean at Selhurst Park during the first-ever League meeting between the two clubs in August 1969. Spurs won 2-0.

1970-1

Tottenham Hotspur enjoyed one of their best-ever seasons in 1970-1. Winners of the Football League Cup, third in the First Division, and into the quarter-finals of the FA Cup, Spurs gave the White Hart Lane fans plenty to cheer about after an indifferent start.

After dropping a point at home to neighbours West Ham on the first day of the new season, Spurs won only twice in their first seven games. But after soundly beating Blackpool at White Hart Lane on 12 September, Tottenham went thirteen matches with only one defeat. In the end the First Division title went to London when Spurs arch-rivals Arsenal clinched it in their very last game — at Tottenham. Ray Kennedy's header in the dying seconds of the match gave the Gunners a 1-0 before almost 52,000 fans with as many locked out of the ground. Spurs had to be content with third spot, thirteen points behind Arsenal and twelve behind runners-up Leeds United.

It was the Football League Cup which gave Spurs glory. The early rounds were fairly easy — wins over Swansea City, Sheffield United, West Brom and Coventry City put them into the semi-final and two legs against Bristol City, then a lowly Second Division team without much hope of stopping Spurs. In fact, City held Spurs 1-1 at Ashton Gate and it was two days before Christmas when the sides met for the return leg at White Hart Lane. After a goalless first-half, Chivers and Pearce won the day for Tottenham.

At one time during the 1970-1 season it looked as though Spurs might be on target for what would have been a unique double of FA Cup and League Cup. Sheffield Wednesday, Carlisle United and Nottingham Forest were each removed from the early stages and when Spurs earned a goalless draw in the sixth round tie against Liverpool at Anfield, all White Hart Lane thought that their side must triumph at home, having done the difficult bit in Liverpool. The reply on 15 March was watched by over 56,000 fans and what an absorbing game they saw. It was not until late in the second-half that Steve Heighway broke the deadlock and scored what proved to be the only goal of the game. It was little consolation for downhearted Tottenham that they had taken part in two thrilling matches which epitomised the very best of cup football.

Earlier, on 27 February 1971, Spurs took the League Cup at Wembley. A crowd of 97,000 paid a record £132,000 to see Spurs and Villa fight for the trophy. The match see-sawed either way before two superb goals late in the game, both scored by Martin Chivers, earned Spurs the cup. It was sad that injury had ruled out Mike England. Indeed, the big Spurs centre-half was not to play again that season after taking the advice of a specialist.

On 4 May, Spurs skipper Alan Mullery asked to be left out of the England party for the Home Internationals and the match with Malta: 'I'm shattered', he told reporters. The following day Tottenham made their first signing for the following season. They paid Burnley a reported record £200,000 for Ralph Coates.

Amidst all the excitement and success of 1970-1 there were one or two embarrassing moments at White Hart Lane. Spurs were among several clubs fined for sending in late details of transfers and

Alan Gilzean – who later scored a goal – in an airborne tussle with Manchester City's George Heslop with Tony Towers looking on. Spurs won 2-0 in this First Division game at White Hart Lane in September 1970.

signings; and the newly-formed Texaco Cup saw Tottenham get no further than the second round where they were beaten on aggregate by Scottish mid-First Division side Motherwell. But they were minor blemishes on an otherwise great season.

Mike England – played in Spurs first twenty-two League matches and was then injured and missed the rest of the season, including the League Cup Final.

First Division Results 1970-1

Aug 15	West Ham Utd	(h)	2-2
(Gilzean 2, 53,640)			
Aug 19	Leeds Utd	(h)	0-2
(39,927)			
Aug 22	Wolves	(a)	3-0
(Mullery, Chivers, Morgan, 23,896)			
Aug 25	Southampton	(a)	0-0
(27,149)			
Aug 29	Coventry City	(h)	1-0
(Chivers 27,103)			
Sep 1	Huddersfield	(a)	1-1
(Chivers, 26,701)			
Sep 5	Arsenal	(a)	0-2
(48,713)			
Sep 12	Blackpool	(h)	3-0
(Mullery, Pen, Peters 2, 19,894)			
Sep 19	Crystal Palace	(a)	3-0
(Mullery, Chivers 2, 41,308)			
Sep 26	Man City	(h)	2-0
(Gilzean, Chivers, 43,490)			
Oct 3	Derby County	(a)	1-1
(Peters, 36,007)			
Oct 10	Liverpool	(h)	1-0
(Peters, 44,457)			
Oct 17	West Ham Utd	(a)	2-2
(Mullery, England, 42,322)			
Oct 24	Stoke City	(h)	3-0
(Gilzean, Chivers 2, 36,238)			
Oct 31	Nottm Forest	(a)	1-0
(Chivers, 25,301)			
Nov 7	Burnley	(h)	4-0
(Gilzean, Perryman, Chivers 2, 30,524)			
Nov 14	Chelsea	(a)	2-0
(Mullery, Pearce, 61,277)			
Nov 21	Newcastle Utd	(h)	1-2
(Chivers, 38,873)			
Nov 28	Everton	(a)	0-0
(43,955)			
Dec 5	Manchester Utd	(h)	2-2
(Peters, Gilzean, 55,693)			
Dec 12	West Brom	(a)	1-3
(Chivers, 26,477)			
Dec 19	Wolves	(h)	0-0
(30,544)			
Jan 9	Leeds United	(a)	2-1
(Chivers 2, 43,907)			

Jan 16   Southampton   (h)   1-3
(Chivers, 39,486)
Jan 30   Everton   (h)   2-1
(Gilzean, Chivers, 42,005)
Feb 6   Manchester Utd   (a)   1-2
(Peters, 48,966)
Feb 17   West Brom   (h)   2-2
(Mullery pen, Gilzean, 22,695)
Feb 20   Newcastle Utd   (a)   0-1
(31,780)
Mar 10   Nottm Forest   (h)   0-1
(21,697)
Mar 13   Chelsea   (h)   2-1
(Peters, Chivers, 49,192)
Mar 20   Burnley   (a)   0-0
(16,332)
Mar 23   Ipswich   (a)   2-1
(Peters, Gilzean, 21,685)
Apr 3   Coventry City   (a)   0-0
(22,947)
Apr 7   Derby County   (h)   2-1
(Pearce, Chivers, 25,627)
Apr 10   Ipswich   (h)   2-0
(Chivers, Morris own goal, 28,708)
Apr 12   Blackpool   (a)   0-0
(16,541)
Apr 17   Liverpool   (a)   0-0
(49,363)
Apr 24   Crystal Palace   (h)   2-0
(Perryman, Blyth own goal 28,619)
Apr 28   Huddersfield   (h)   1-1
(Chivers, 18,859)
May 1   Man. City   (a)   1-0
(Perryman, 19,764)
May 2   Arsenal   (h)   0-1
(51,992)
May 5   Stoke City   (a)   1-0
(Peters, 14,000)

Final League Record

P42, W19, D14, L9, F54, A33, Pts 52, Pos 3rd

League Goalscorers: Chivers 21, Gilzean 9,
Peters 9, Mullery 6, Perryman 3, Pearce 2,
England 1, Morgan 1, own goals 2

FA Cup
Jan 2   Sheffield Wed   (h)   4-1
(Round 3)
(Peters, Gilzean 2, Mullery, 34,170)
Jan 23   Carlisle Utd   (a)   3-2
(Round 4)
(Gilzean, Peters, Neighbour, 25,400)
Feb 13   Nottm. Forest   (h)   2-1
(Round 5)
(Chivers, Gilzean, 46,366)

Mar 6   Liverpool   (a)   0-0
(Round 6)
(54,731)
Mar 15   Liverpool   (h)   0-1
(replay)
(56,283)
FA Cup goalscorers: Gilzean 4, Peters 2,
Chivers 1, Mullery 1, Neighbour 1

Football League Cup
Sep 9   Swansea City   (h)   3-0
(Round 2)
(Peters, Morgan, Perryman, 15,848)
Oct 7   Sheffield Utd   (h)   2-1
(Round 3)
(Pearce, Chivers, 23,559)
Oct 28   West Brom   (h)   5-0
(Round 4)
(Peters, Gilzean 2, 31,598)
Nov 18   Coventry City   (h)   4-1
(Round 5)
(Chivers 3, Gilzean, 31,864)
Dec 16   Bristol City   (a)   1-1
(SF 1st leg)
(Gilzean 30,002)
Dec 23   Bristol City   (h)   2-0
(SF 2nd leg)
(Chivers, Pearce 29,982) Spurs won 3-1 on
aggregate)
Feb 27   Aston Villa   (W)   2-0
                                (= Wembley)
(Final)
(Chivers 2, 97,000)
League Cup goalscorers: Chivers 7, Gilzean 4,
Peters 4, Pearce 2, Perryman 1, Morgan 1

Texaco Cup
Sep 16   Dunfermline   (h)   4-0
(Round 1 first leg)
(Chivers 3, England 16,388)
Sep 29   Dunfermline   (a)   3-0
(Round 1 second leg)
(Peters 2, Chivers, 9,000) Spurs won 7-0 on
aggregate.
Oct 21   Motherwell   (h)   3-2
(Round 2 first leg)
(Chivers, Peters 2, 19,570)
Nov 3   Motherwell   (a)   1-3
(Round 2 second leg)
(Pearce, 30,000) Spurs lost 4-5 on aggregate
Texaco Cup goalscorers: Chivers 5, Peters 4,
Pearce 1, England 1

1971-2

This was one of Spurs best-ever seasons and their 1971-2 record speaks for itself — UEFA Cup winners, semi-finalists in the Football League Cup, quarter-finalists in the FA Cup, and sixth place in the First Division is as magnificent a record as any English club can boast over the years.

Tottenham started magnificently. By the end of October they had played fourteen games and lost only three in the First Division. With Martin Chivers regularly finding the back of the net, Spurs at one time looked as though they might well take the First Division championship, and at the end of the season, Chivers had scored twenty-five goals in league matches alone to underline his worth as one of the most dangerous marksmen in the First Division.

But it was in cup football that Spurs made their mark in 1971-2. Their run started on 8 September when they beat West Brom 1-0 at the Hawthorns in the second round of the League Cup. Torquay United were efficiently removed 4-1 at Plainmoor and although Preston North End held Tottenham to a 1-1 draw in London, Chivers and Perryman gave Spurs a fifth round tie when the two sides met at Deepdale.

After Blackpool had been disposed of 2-0 — Tottenham's first home win of their Football League run that season — Spurs faced Chelsea in an all-London semi-final and after losing the first leg 3-2, they could only manage a 2-2 draw at home to allow Chelsea to go through to the final, 5-4 on aggregate. Their games had been watched by a total exceeding 230,000 spectators.

Martin Peters scored twice as Spurs hammered Nottingham Forest 6-1 in October 1971.

In the FA Cup Tottenham Hotspur fared almost as well, although they had a nasty shock when Carlisle United sneaked a 1-1 draw at White Hart Lane in the third round before being beaten 3-1 at Brunton Park. Rotherham United were Spurs next opponents and they went down 2-0 at White Hart Lane before Spurs faced Everton in the fifth round at Goodison Park. Over 50,000 Everton fans — and not a few Spurs supporters — saw Tottenham win 2-0 with goals from Gilzean and Peters, and march on to a sixth round match with Leeds United. It was here that Spurs interest in the 1971-2 FA Cup came to an end. Allan Clarke and Jack Charlton scored goals which sent the Yorkshire club to Wembley.

But Spurs had a third crack at cup football in 1971-2 and it proved to be third time lucky. Spurs had qualified for the UEFA Cup and a staggering 15-1 aggregate against Keflavik, the champions of Iceland, signalled the way ahead for Tottenham. France's champions, Nantes, and the Rumanians of Rapid Bucharest were other Tottenham victims and in the quarter-finals, Spurs faced a further Rumanian challenge in the form of UT Arad. Morgan and England gave Spurs a valuable 2-0 win in Rumania and although the Arad side managed a creditable 1-1 draw at White Hart Lane, the away win was enough to send Spurs into the semi-final where they met and beat AC Milan — the second leg a 1-1 draw in San Siro Stadium. That left just Wolverhampton Wanderers between Spurs and the first-ever UEFA Cup — the old-style Fairs Cup was abolished at the end of 1970-1 — and after winning 2-1 at Molineaux Spurs had set themselves up for a fine end to the season. A 1-1 draw at White Hart Lane ensured that the name of Tottenham Hotspur would be the first on the new trophy.

First Division Results 1971-2

Aug 16 Wolves (a) 2-2
(Chivers, Gilzean 30,465)

Aug 18 Newcastle Utd (h) 0-0
(42,715)

Aug 21 Huddersfield T (h) 4-1
(Chivers 2, Gilzean 2, 33,260)

Aug 25 Leeds Utd (a) 1-0
(Gilzean 25,099)

Aug 28 Man City (a) 0-4
(33,683)

Sep 4 Liverpool (h) 2-0
(Chivers, Peters 50,124)

Sep 11 Sheffield United (a) 2-2
(Peters, Gilzean 41,112)

Sep 18 Crystal Palace (h) 3-0
(Peters pen, Chivers, Mullery 37,239)

Sep 25 Coventry City (a) 0-1
(26,302)

Oct 2 Ipswich Town (h) 2-1
(Chivers, Peters 33,562)

Oct 9 Derby County (a) 2-2
(Chivers, Pearce 35,774)

Oct 16 Wolves (h) 4-1
(Gilzean, Chivers 2, Neighbour 36,582)

Oct 23 Nottm Forest (h) 6-1
(Peters 2 (1 pen) Chivers, Mullery, Pearce 2 35,746)

Oct 30 Stoke City (a) 0-2
(28,343)

Nov 6 Everton (h) 3-0
(Pratt, Chivers 2 40,005)

Nov 13 Man United (a) 1-3
(Chivers 54,000)

Nov 20 West Brom (h) 3-2
(England, Gilzean 2 31,895)

Nov 24 Arsenal (h) 1-1
(Chivers 52,884)

Nov 27 Chelsea (a) 0-1
(52,581)

Dec 4 Southampton (h) 1-0
(Gilzean 31,351)

Dec 11 Leicester C (a) 1-0
(Peters 30,721)

Dec 18 Liverpool (a) 0-0
(43,409)

Dec 27 West Ham Utd (h) 0-1
(53,888)

Jan 1 Crystal Palace (a) 1-1
(Chivers 35,841)

Jan 8 Man City (h) 1-1
(Peters 36,470)

Jan 22 Newcastle Utd (a) 1-3
(Gilzean 29,950)

Jan 29 Leeds Utd (h) 1-0
(Chivers 46,774)

Feb 12 Nottm Forest (a) 1-0
(Peters 20,209)

Feb 19 Stoke City (h) 2-0
(Chivers 2 32,841)

Mar 1 Everton (a) 1-1
(Peters 21,601)

Mar 4 Man United (h) 2-0
(Perryman, Chivers 54,814)

Mar 11 Derby County (h) 0-1
(36,310)

Mar 25 Sheffield Utd (h) 2-0
(Chivers, Gilzean 30,984)

Mar 28 Huddersfield T (a) 1-1
(Pearce 16,023)

Mar 31 Coventry City (h) 1-0
(Chivers 32,548)

Apr 1 West Ham Utd (a) 0-2
(30,763)

Apr 3 Ipswich Town (a) 1-2
(Chivers 24,200)

Apr 8 West Brom (a) 1-1
(Chivers 20,860)

Apr 15 Chelsea (h) 3-0
(Chivers 2, Coates 45,799)

Apr 22 Southampton (a) 0-0
(24,914)

Apr 29 Leicester City (h) 4-3
(England, Pearce, Knowles 2, (1 pen) 19,631

May 11 Arsenal (a) 2-0
(Mullery, Coates 42,038)

Final League record
P42, W19, D13, L10, F63, A42, Pts 51,
Pos 6th

Football League goalscorers: Chivers 25,
Gilzean 11, Peters 10, Pearce 5, Mullery 3,
England 2, Coates 2, Knowles 2, Pratt 1,
Perryman 1, Neighbour 1

FA Cup

Jan 15 Carlisle Utd (h) 1-1
(Round 3)
(Gilzean 33,702)

Jan 18 Carlisle Utd (a) 3-1
(replay)
(Chivers 2, Gilzean 21,560)

Feb 5 Rotherham Utd (h) 2-0
(Round 4)
(Gilzean, Peters 36,903)

Feb 26 Everton (a) 2-0
(Round 5)
(Gilzean, Peters 50,511)

Mar 18 Leeds United (a) 1-2
(Round 6)
(Pratt 43,937)

FA Cup goalscorers: Gilzean 4, Chivers 2,
Peters 2, Pratt

Alan Mullery holds the UEFA Cup after Spurs beat Wolves in a two-legged final.

Football League Cup

Sep 8   West Brom   (a)   1-0
(Round 2)
(Pearce   26,200)
Oct 6   Torquay U   (a)   4-1
(Round 3)
(Peters pen, Chivers 2, Pearce   20,100)
Oct 27   Preston NE   (h)   1-1
(Round 4)
(Chivers   30,338)
Nov 8   Preston NE   (a)   2-1
(replay)
(Chivers, Perryman   28,000)
Nov 17   Blackpool   (h)   2-0
(Round 5)
(Peters, Chivers   30,019)
Dec 22   Chelsea   (a)   2-3
(SF 1st leg)
(Naylor, Chivers   43,330)
Jan 5   Chelsea   (h)   2-2
(SF 2nd leg)
(Chivers, Peters pen 52,755) Spurs lost 4-5 on aggregate

Football League Cup goalscorers: Chivers 7, Peters 3, Pearce 2, Naylor 1, Perryman 1

UEFA Cup

Sep 14   Keflavik   (a)   6-1
(1st Rd 1st leg)
(Gilzean 3, Coates 2, Mullery 2 5,000)
Sep 28   Keflavik   (h)   9-0
(1st Rd 2nd leg)
(Chivers 3, Perryman, Coates, Knowles, Gilzean 2, Holder   23,818)

Oct 20   Nantes   (a)   0-0
(2nd Rd 1st leg)
(18,000)
Nov 2   Nantes   (h)   1-0
(2nd Rd 2nd leg)
(Peters   32,630)
Dec 8   Bucharest   (h)   3-0
(3rd Rd 1st leg)
(Peters, Chivers 2 30,702)
Dec 15   Bucharest   (a)   2-0
(3rd Rd 2nd leg)
(Pearce, Chivers   25,000)
Mar 7   UT Arad   (a)   2-0
(QF 1st leg)
(Morgan, England   20,000)
Mar 21   UT Arad   (h)   1-1
(QF 2nd leg)
(Gilzean   30,253)
Apr 4   AC Milan   (h)   2-1
(SF 1st leg)
(Perryman 2   42,064)
Apr 16   AC Milan   (a)   1-1
(SF 2nd leg)
(Mullery   80,000)
May 3   Wolves   (a)   2-1
(Final 1st leg)
(Chivers 2   38,362)
May 17   Wolves   (h)   1-1
(Final 2nd leg)
(Mullery   53,000)

UEFA Cup goalscorers: Chivers 8, Gilzean 6, Mullery 4, Perryman 3, Coates 2, Peters 2, Holder 1, Morgan 1, Pearce 1, Knowles 1, England 1

1972-3

Tottenham Hotspur went marching back to Wembley for the second successive year to retain the Football League Cup. White Hart Lane fans were back on the glory trail as Spurs beat Norwich City in an unmemorable final to retain the trophy. But there was plenty of cup excitement in other competitions as well, although Spurs were not always on the right side of it. After non-Leaguers Margate had gone crashing 6-0 in the third round of the FA Cup, Tottenham survived a gruelling fourth round tie at Derby's Baseball Ground to draw 1-1. In the replay, Spurs were seemingly coasting 3-1 with ten minutes to play when Roger Davies scored two sensational goals to pull Derby back to 3-3. The big striker went on to complete his hat-trick and in extra-time Spurs were out of the FA Cup, beaten 5-3 in one of London's most thrilling ties.

Spurs had already reached the League Cup Final for the second year running. Although they beat Huddersfield in the second round, Spurs faced sterner Yorkshire opposition when they met Middlesbrough and it took three games before Spurs were through. Less than 20,000 watched the third match at White Hart Lane on 30 October.

After sweeping past Millwall in the next round, Spurs faced further difficulties against Liverpool in the fifth round. At Anfield the match ended 1-1 when Peters scored a vital goal; and at White Hart Lane it was Chivers again, this time with two goals, who saw Tottenham safely home 3-1. Peters and Pratt scored the goals which gave Spurs a 2-1 win in the Molineux leg of the semi-final. The second leg was due to be staged on New Year's Day but after complaints from both managers, the Football League took the unusual step of allowing the clubs to postpone their League games and meet on a Saturday — 30 December. At White Hart Lane, Wolves reversed the 2-1 scoreline and it took a 111th minute goal by Chivers before Spurs were on the Wembley trail again.

The final against Ron Saunders' Norwich City was a shabby affair, in no way living up to the backcloth of Wembley Stadium. The only goal of the game came with just eighteen minutes to play. Ralph Coates, who had come on for the injured John Pratt after twenty-two minutes, cracked the ball home from just eight yards out after a long throw from Chivers had flown to him via a tackle on

Peters by a Norwich defender. Both Knowles and Pearce hit the post either side of Coates's goal, but Norwich might have dragged the game out of the fire when centre-half Duncan Forbes headed wide of an open Spurs goal. The game was fought in midfield with Spurs denied the chance to express themselves. Even so, they now had the unique record of nine major finals and nine victories.

Spurs also met Liverpool in the semi-final of the UEFA Cup in 1972-3 but the outcome was not to Tottenham's benefit. After removing the Norwegian, Greek, Yugoslavian and Portuguese representatives, Spurs could feel pleased at trailing only 1-0 after the Anfield leg of the semi-final. But although they won 2-1 at White Hart Lane, it was not enough and Steve Heighway's goal sent Liverpool to the final on the away goals rule.

In the First Division, Tottenham rose as high as third during the season but had to be content with eighth place in the final analysis. There was one other moment of celebration at White Hart Lane in 1972-3 when Pat Jennings was elected Footballer of the Year. It had been a fine season for Spurs.

Alan Gilzean is back in the Spurs defence clearing from West Brom's Alistair Robertson during the 1-1 draw at White Hart Lane in November 1972.

First Division results 1972-3

Aug 12   Coventry City   (h)   2-0
(Peters 2, 33,884)

Aug 16   West Brom   (a)   1-0
(Peters 19,344)

Aug 19   Wolves   (a)   2-3
(Peters, Pratt 24,237)

Aug 23   Birmingham C   (h)   2-0
(Chivers, Coates 30,798)

Aug 26   Leeds United   (h)   0-0
(41,191)

Aug 30   Newcastle Utd   (a)   1-0
(Kinnear 27,500)

Sep 2   Ipswich   (a)   1-1
(Peters pen 23,160)

Sep 9   Crystal Palace   (h)   2-1
(Peters pen, England 28,545)

Sep 16   Man City   (a)   1-2
(Peters 31,713)

Sep 23   West Ham Utd   (h)   1-0
(Lampard own goal 51,700)

Sep 30   Derby County   (a)   1-2
(Perryman 32,133)

Oct 7   Stoke City   (h)   4-3
(Pratt 2, Gilzean, Smith own goal 31,951)

Oct 14   Norwich City   (a)   1-2
(Chivers 34,555)

Oct 21   Chelsea   (h)   0-1
(47,429)

Oct 28   Man Utd   (a)   4-1
(Peters 4 52,497)

Nov 4   Birmingham City   (a)   0-0
(38,504)

Nov 11   West Brom   (h)   1-1
(Chivers 21,875)

Nov 18   Leicester City   (a)   1-0
(Chivers 22,707)

Nov 25   Liverpool   (h)   1-2
(Chivers 45,399)

Dec 2   Southampton   (a)   1-1
(Chivers 16,486)

Dec 9   Arsenal   (h)   1-2
(Peters 47,505)

Dec 16   Everton   (a)   1-3
(Neighbour 31,190)

Dec 23   Sheffield Utd   (h)   2-0
(Chivers, Perryman 19,577)

Dec 26   West Ham Utd   (a)   2-2
(Pearce, Peters 37,397)

Jan 6   Leeds Utd   (a)   1-2
(Gilzean 32,404)

Jan 20   Ipswich   (h)   0-1
(33,014)

Jan 27   Crystal Palace   (a)   0-0
(44,531)

Feb 10   Man City   (h)   2-3
(Chivers 2 30,944)

Feb 17   Coventry City   (a)   1-0
(Pratt 26,795)

Feb 24   Everton   (h)   3-0
(Chivers, Gilzean, Pearce 27,427)

Mar 10   Norwich City   (h)   3-0
(Pearce, Chivers 2 (1 pen) 25,081)

Mar 14   Stoke City   (a)   1-1
(Pearce 23,351)

Mar 24   Man Utd   (h)   1-1
(Chivers 49,751)

Mar 31   Liverpool   (a)   1-1
(Gilzean 48,477)

Apr 3   Chelsea   (a)   1-0
(Pratt 25,536)

Apr 7   Southampton   (h)   1-2
(Peters 23,693)

Apr 14   Arsenal   (a)   1-1
(Chivers 50,863)

Apr 20   Derby County   (h)   1-0
(McFarland own goal 22,639)

Apr 21   Leicester City   (h)   1-1
(Gilzean 22,712)

Apr 28   Newcastle Utd   (h)   3-2
(Chivers 2 (1 pen), Peters 21,721)

Apr 30   Wolves   (h)   2-2
(Coates, Collins 16,941)

May 2   Sheffield Utd   (a)   2-3
(Chivers pen, Collins 20,716)

Final League Record

P42, W16, D13, L13, F58, A48, Pts 45, Pos 8

League goalscorers: Chivers 17, Peters 15, Pratt 5, Gilzean 5, Pearce 4, Coates 2, Perryman 2, Collins 2, Kinnear 1, England 1, Neighbour 1, own goals 3

FA Cup

Jan 13   Margate   (a)   6-0
(Round 3)
(Chivers 2, Pearce, Peters, Pratt, Knowles 8,500)

Feb 3   Derby County   (a)   1-1
(Round 4)
(Chivers 37,895)

Feb 7   Derby County   (h)   3-5
(replay)
(Chivers, Gilzean, England pen. 52,736)
After extra-time

FA Cup goalscorers: Chivers 4, Pearce, Peters, Knowles, Pratt, Gilzean, England

Football League Cup

Sep 6   Huddersfield   (h)   2-1
(Round 2)
(Chivers, Gilzean 21,422)
Oct 3   Middlesbrough   (a)   1-1
(Round 3)
(Pearce 23,822)
Oct 11   Middlesbrough   (h)   0-0
(19,256) After extra-time
Oct 30   Middlesbrough   (h)   2-1
(2nd replay)
(Peters, Gilzean 19,287)
Nov 1   Millwall   (h)   2-0
(Round 4)
(Peters, Perryman 27,904)
Dec 4   Liverpool   (a)   1-1
(Round 5)
(Peters 48,677)
Dec 6   Liverpool   (h)   3-1
(replay)
(Chivers 2, Pratt 34,565)
Dec 20   Wolves   (a)   2-1
(SF 1st leg)
(Peters, Pratt 28,357)
Dec 30   Wolves   (h)   2-2
(SF 2nd leg)
(Peters, Chivers 41,716) After extra-time.
Spurs won 4-3 on aggregate
Mar 3   Norwich C   (W)   1-0
(Coates 100,000)   (Final)

Football League Cup goalscorers: Peters 5, Chivers 4, Gilzean 2, Pratt 2, Perryman, Pearce, Coates

UEFA Cup

Sep 13   Lynn Oslo   (a)   6-3
(1st Rd 1st leg)
(Peters, Pratt, Gilzean 2, Chivers 2 10,777)
Sep 27   Lynn Oslo   (h)   6-0
(1st Rd 2nd leg)
(Chivers 3, Pearce, Coates 2 21,088) Spurs won 12-3 on aggregate
Oct 25   Olympiakos Piraeus   (h)   4-0
(2nd Rd 1st leg)
(Pearce 2, Chivers, Coates 27,860)
Nov 8   Olympiakos Piraeus   (a)   0-1
(2nd Rd 2nd leg)
(40,000) Spurs won 4-1 on aggregate
Nov 29   Red Star Belgrade   (h)   2-0
(3rd Rd 1st leg)
(Chivers, Gilzean 23,958)
Dec 13   Red Star Belgrade   (a)   0-1
(3rd Rd 2nd leg)
(75,000) Spurs won 2-1 on aggregate
Mar 7   Setubal   (h)   1-0
(Rd 4 1st leg)
(Evans 30,469)
Mar 21   Setubal   (a)   1-2
(Rd 4 2nd leg)
(Chivers 30,000) Spurs won on away goals
Apr 10   Liverpool   (a)   0-1
(SF 1st leg)
(42,174)
Apr 25   Liverpool   (h)   2-1
(SF 2nd leg)
(Peters 2 46,919) Spurs lost on away goals

UEFA Cup goalscorers: Chivers 8, Coates 3, Gilzean 3, Pearce 3, Peters 3, Evans 1, Pratt 1

Spurs beat Stoke 4-3 in October 1972 and Alan Gilzean, scorer of Spurs second goal, tussles here with Stoke's centre-half Denis Smith.

1973-4

If ever there was a season of mixed fortunes in the history of Tottenham Hotspur Football Club, it was in 1973-4. See-sawing about the middle of the First Division before finally finishing in eleventh place, the club was also knocked out of the FA Cup and the Football League Cup — both at the first attempt. Yet in the UEFA Cup, Spurs went all the way to the final and almost took the trophy they first won in 1972.

In the league, Spurs started indifferently, losing to a Mick Coop goal at Coventry on the first day of the season before winning 2-1 at St Andrews the following Tuesday when Martin Peters scored both goals against Birmingham City. Spurs delight was short-lived, however, and in the first home match, Billy Bremner (2) and Allan Clarke saw Leeds to a crushing 3-0 win at White Hart Lane and Spurs down to nineteenth place with the season only one week old.

A home defeat at the hands of Burnley in mid-week was followed by a 1-0 win over West Ham United at Upton Park and after fourteen days of the 1973-4 campaign, the trend was set with Spurs slipping up at home one week and then pulling off some creditable wins away from White Hart Lane. There were home defeats by Sheffield United, Newcastle and Wolverhampton Wanderers; and away points at Burnley, Ipswich, Norwich, Everton and Southampton. By the turn of the year Spurs were in fifteenth place. Not in danger of relegation — but not in danger of winning the title either. In addition, Spurs — the holders — were knocked out of the Football League Cup at the first hurdle when Eire international Don Givens gave QPR a 1-0 win in the second round match at Loftus road.

There had also been transfer speculation at Tottenham during the first half of the season. First Bill Nicholson had turned down a transfer request from Joe Kinnear — despite the fact that the Irishman was to play in only seven league matches (four of those as substitute); and then Spurs set up an exchange deal with Manchester City which fell through when Rodney Marsh declined to change places with Martin Chivers.

With the whole country gripped in a State of Emergency through power cuts, football kicked-off earlier, played on midweek afternoons, and even on Sundays — although Spurs staged no Sunday games at White Hart Lane. Steve Earle of Leicester City ended Spurs interest in the FA Cup as early as the third round and, with Tottenham coasting to a mid-table position in the First Division, it was the UEFA Cup which led Tottenham fans to think that

Martin Chivers just fails to reach a loose ball and Paul Reaney and David Harvey of Leeds United breathe again. Leeds hammered Tottenham 3-0 on 1 September 1973.

One week later Spurs beat West Ham United 1-0 at Upton Park. Here Ray Evans tackles Hammers Ted MacDougal and the United player had to go off for treatment before being substituted by Holland.

there might be some hope yet in 1973-4.

A big 9-2 aggregate win over Grasshoppers Zurich of Switzerland saw Spurs into the second round and two ties with Scotland's Aberdeen, who were duly removed 5-2. Dynamo Tbilisi of Russia and Cologne of West Germany were next to fall; and in the semi-finals, East Germany's Lokomotiv Leipzig paved the way for a two-legged final against the Dutch masters, Feyenoord. Mike England and an own goal by Van Daele earned Spurs a 2-2 draw at White Hart Lane but this was insufficient and Rijsbergen and Ressel made it 4-2 on aggregate in Rotterdam where Spurs fans caused havoc. Seventy so-called Tottenham 'supporters' were arrested and over 200 people injured as Bill Nicholson broadcast an appeal to them: 'You hooligans are a disgrace to Tottenham Hotspur and a disgrace to English football. This is football — not a war!' The season had ended on a bitter note.

First Division results 1973-4

Aug 25	Coventry City	(a)	0-1	(24,712)
Aug 28	Birmingham (Peters 2	(a)	2-1	37,754)
Sep 1	Leeds United	(h)	0-3	(42,801)
Sep 5	Burnley (Knowles, Chivers	(h)	2-3	25,543)
Sep 8	West Ham Utd (Chivers	(a)	1-0	30,888)
Sep 11	Burnley (Holder, Peters	(a)	2-2	25,078)
Sep 15	Sheffield U (Chivers	(h)	1-2	26,350)
Sep 22	Liverpool (Peters, Chivers	(a)	2-3	42,901)
Sep 29	Derby County (Coates	(h)	1-0	30,408)
Oct 6	Ipswich	(a)	0-0	(23,903)
Oct 13	Arsenal (Gilzean, Chivers	(h)	2-0	41,856)
Oct 20	Norwich City (Gilzean	(a)	1-1	25,032)
Oct 27	Newcastle Utd	(h)	0-2	(31,259)
Nov 3	Everton (Perryman	(a)	1-1	37,827)
Nov 10	Man United (Chivers, Knowles	(h)	2-1	42,756)
Nov 17	Southampton (Chivers	(a)	1-1	22,827)
Nov 24	Wolves (Chivers pen,	(h)	1-3	23,541)
Dec 1	Leicester	(a)	0-3	(22,088)
Dec 8	Stoke (Evans, Pratt	(h)	2-1	14,034)
Dec 15	Man City	(h)	0-2	(17,066)
Dec 22	Derby County	(a)	0-2	(23,672)
Dec 26	QPR	(h)	0-0	(30,762)
Dec 29	West Ham Utd (Pratt, Chivers	(h)	2-0	33,176)
Jan 1	Leeds United (McGrath	(a)	1-1	46,545)
Jan 12	Sheffield U (Coates, McGrath	(a)	2-2	20,368)
Jan 19	Coventry C (Peters 2	(h)	2-1	20,985)
Feb 2	Man City	(a)	0-0	(24,652)
Feb 6	Birmingham (Chivers 3, Dillon	(h)	4-2	14,345)
Feb 16	Arsenal (McGrath	(a)	1-0	38,804)
Feb 23	Ipswich T (Pratt	(h)	1-1	26,289)
Mar 2	QPR (Chivers pen,	(a)	1-3	25,775)
Mar 16	Norwich City	(h)	0-0	(18,466)
Mar 23	Man United (Coates	(a)	1-0	36,278)
Mar 30	Everton	(h)	0-2	(19,849)
Apr 3	Chelsea (Evans	(h)	1-2	23,646)
Apr 6	Wolves (McGrath	(a)	1-1	24,073)
Apr 13	Southampton (Chivers 2, Pratt	(h)	3-1	21,456)
Apr 15	Chelsea	(a)	0-0	(26,258)
Apr 20	Stoke	(a)	0-1	(20,189)
Apr 27	Leicester (Chivers	(h)	1-0	20,110)
May 8	Liverpool (McGrath	(h)	1-1	24,618)
May 11	Newcastle Utd (Chivers, Gilzean	(a)	2-0	20,000)

Final League Record
P42, W14, D14, L14, F45, A50, Pts 42, Pos 11

League goalscorers: Chivers 17, Peters 6, McGrath 5, Pratt 4, Coates 3, Gilzean 3, Knowles 2, Evans 2, Holder 1, Perryman 1, Dillon 1

FA Cup
Jan 5   Leicester C   (a)   0-1
(Round 3)
(28,280)

UEFA Cup
Sep 19   Grasshoppers   (a)   5-1
(1st Rd 1st leg)
(Chivers 2, Gilzean 2, Evans   11,000)
Oct 3   Grasshoppers   (h)   4-1
(1st Rd 2nd leg)
(Peters 2, England, opp. own goal 18,105)
Oct 24   Aberdeen   (a)   1-1

(2nd Rd 1st leg)
(Coates 30,000)
Nov 7   Aberdeen   (h)   4-1
(2nd Rd 2nd leg)
(Peters, Neighbour, McGrath 2 21,785)
Nov 28   Tbilisi   (a)   1-1
(3rd Rd 1st leg)
(Coates 42,000)
Dec 12   Tbilisi   (h)   5-1
(3rd Rd 2nd leg)
(McGrath, Chivers 2, Peters 2 20,000)

Football League Cup
Oct 8   QPR   (a)   0-1
(Round 2)
(23,353)

Mar 3   Cologne   (a)   2-1
(4th Rd 1st leg)
(McGrath, Peters 28,000)
Mar 20   Cologne   (h)   3-0
(4th Rd 2nd leg)
(Chivers, Coates, Peters 40,968)
Apr 10   Lok Leipzig   (a)   2-1
(SF 1st leg)
(Peters, McGrath 74,000)
Apr 24   Lok Leipzig   (h)   2-0
(SF 2nd leg)
(McGrath, Chivers 41,280)
May 21   Feyenoord   (h)   2-2
(Final 1st leg)
(England, opposition own goal 46,281)
May 29   Feyenoord   (a)   0-2
(Final 2nd leg)
(68,000) Spurs lost 2-4 on aggregate
UEFA Cup goalscorers: Peters 8, Chivers 6, McGrath 6, Coates 3, Gilzean 2, England 2, Evans 1, Neighbour 1, opposition own goal 2

1974-5

The start of the 1974-5 season was disastrous for Tottenham Hotspur. An opening day defeat at home when Ipswich Town won 1-0 at White Hart Lane through Johnson was followed by two more reverses with exactly the same scoreline. And although Martin Peters finally broke Spurs duck in the fourth match of the season — at home to Manchester City — Tottenham were still pointless as City scored twice. That was on 28 August and Spurs were bottom of the table with a record of P4; W0; D0; L4; For1; Against5. The following day, manager Bill Nicholson resigned, ending an association with the club which went back thirty-nine years as player and team boss, sixteen of them as manager.

Fifty-four-year-old Nicholson had some strong things to say when his resignation was made public: 'Players are becoming impossible. They all talk about security and yet they are not prepared to work for it. They no longer have respect and I am abused by the players when they come to talk to me.' Nicholson also stated that he was unable to sign players for Spurs because the club refused to give in to their demands for under-the-counter payments. 'The minimum backhander in the London area is supposed to be £7,000 tax free. There is no way that I will be party to that sort of thing.' That weekend, Jimmy Neighbour's two goals gave Spurs their first points of the season when Derby

County — the team which would eventually win the title — went down 2-0 at White Hart Lane. Afterwards, Martin Peters and Phil Beal led a deputation asking Nicholson to stay. But his mind was made up and new names were bandied around for the vacant position, including those of Danny Blanchflower and the Hull City manager and former Arsenal centre-half, Terry Neill.

On 11 September, Neill was appointed when Hull gave Spurs permission to approach the man who was also team manager of the Northern Ireland international side and he came to White Hart Lane to sign a five-year contract. He warned players and fans: 'I admire Bill Nicholson greatly — but I am my own man.' On the day that his appointment was announced, Neill had the unpleasant news that Spurs had been thrashed 4-0 at home by Middlesbrough in the second round of the Football League Cup. He was facing a daunting challenge. The previous Saturday, Spurs had lost 5-2 at Liverpool and were still firmly entrenched at the foot of the First Division.

Even successive wins over West Ham and Wolves could not disperse the White Hart Lane gloom which seemed to be spreading over North London. On 5 October, Spurs lost 3-2 at home to Burnley before 18,000 fans and they were next-to-bottom of the table. Only Arsenal were below them. The following week, Chelsea won 1-0 at Stamford Bridge to send Spurs right back to the bottom and when unfashionable Carlisle United came to London they managed a 1-1 draw with Spurs in front of less than 13,000 spectators. It was becoming increasingly obvious that Spurs were struggling desperately for survival.

On 17 October, Spurs signed striker John Duncan from Dundee for a reported fee of £125,000 and two weeks later the Scotsman repaid some of that fee with both goals in Spurs 2-2 away draw with Stoke. Things began to look brighter. Martin Chivers came off the transfer list and signed a four-year contract with Spurs and a 3-0 win over Newcastle lifted Tottenham to fifteenth place by 7 December.

But the New Year was one of struggle. Out of the FA Cup after losing a home third round replay with Forest, Spurs fought gamely on with Duncan hitting priceless goals in the battle against relegation. But it was not until the last day of the season that they missed the drop by just one point. Spurs beat Leeds 4-2 with a goal from Martin Chivers — in his first game for two months!

◄ *Wolves Mike Bailey gets a foot to the ball as Martin Chivers and Martin Peters break through. Chivers scored twice and Peters once as Spurs won 3-2 at Molineux in September 1974.*

QPR's Don Givens outjumps Phil Beal as Rangers beat Spurs 2-1 at White Hart Lane in December 1974. ►

First Division results 1974-5

Date	Opponent		Score
Aug 17	Ipswich Town	(h)	0-1
(26,344)			
Aug 21	Man City	(a)	0-1
(31,549)			
Aug 24	Carlisle Utd	(a)	0-1
(18,426)			
Aug 28	Man City	(h)	1-2
(Peters 20,079)			
Aug 31	Derby County	(h)	2-0
(Neighbour 2 20,770)			
Sep 7	Liverpool	(a)	2-5
(Perryman, Chivers 47,538)			
Sep 14	West Ham Utd	(h)	2-1
(England, Chivers 27,959)			
Sep 21	Wolves	(a)	3-2
(Peters, Chivers 2 20,647)			
Sep 28	Middlesbrough	(h)	1-2
(Neighbour 23,285)			
Oct 5	Burnley	(h)	2-3
(Pratt, England 18441)			
Oct 12	Chelsea	(a)	0-1
(32,660)			
Oct 16	Carlisle Utd	(h)	1-1
(Chivers 12,823)			
Oct 19	Arsenal	(h)	2-0
(Perryman, Chivers 36,194)			
Oct 26	Luton Town	)a)	1-1
(Chivers 22,420)			
Nov 2	Stoke City	(a)	2-2
(Duncan 2 24,668)			
Nov 9	Everton	(h)	1-1
(Chivers 28,952)			
Nov 16	Leicester City	(a)	2-1
(Peters, Coates, 23,244)			
Nov 23	Birmingham City	(h)	0-0
(27,761)			
Nov 30	Sheffield Utd	(a)	1-0
(Duncan 20,289)			
Dec 4	Leeds United	(a)	1-2
(Duncan 25,832)			
Dec 7	Newcastle Utd	(h)	3-0
(Bell own goal, Chivers, Knowles 23,422)			
Dec 14	Ipswich Town	(a)	0-4
(20,829)			
Dec 21	QPR	(h)	1-2
(Duncan 21,150)			
Dec 26	West Ham Utd	(h)	1-1
(Peters 37,682)			
Dec 28	Coventry City	(h)	1-1
(Smith own goal 20,307)			
Jan 11	Newcastle Utd	(a)	5-2
(Conn 3, Knowles, Duncan 38,270)			
Jan 18	Sheffield Utd	(h)	1-3
(Duncan 15,812)			
Feb 1	Everton	(a)	0-1
(40,912)			
Feb 8	Stoke City	(h)	0-2
(22,894)			
Feb 15	Coventry City	(a)	1-1
(Duncan 14,891)			
Feb 18	Birmingham City	(a)	0-1
(24,240)			
Feb 22	Leicester City	(h)	0-3
(20,937)			
Mar 1	Derby County	(a)	1-3
(Jones 23,000)			
Mar 15	Middlesbrough	(a)	0-3
(25,182)			
Mar 22	Liverpool	(h)	0-2
(34,331)			
Mar 28	Wolves	(h)	3-0
(Duncan, Perryman 2 27,238)			
Mar 29	QPR	(a)	1-0
(Duncan 25,461)			
Apr 5	Luton Town	(h)	2-1
(Duncan, Conn 25,796)			
Apr 12	Burnley	(a)	2-3
(Duncan, Perryman 17,860)			
Apr 19	Chelsea	(h)	2-0
(Perryman, Conn 51,064)			
Apr 26	Arsenal	(a)	0-1
(43,752)			
Apr 28	Leeds Utd	(h)	4-2
(Knowles 2 (1 pen), Chivers, Conn 49,886)			

Final League Record
P42. W13, D8, L21, F52, A63, Pts 34, Pos 19th

League goalscorers: Duncan 12, Chivers 10, Conn 6, Perryman 6, Peters 4, Knowles 4, Neighbour 3, England 2, Pratt 1, Coates 1, Jones 1, Own goals 2

FA Cup

Date	Opponent		Score
Jan 3	Nottm Forest	(a)	1-1
(Round 3)			
(Chivers 23,355)			
Jan 8	Nottm Forest	(h)	0-1
(replay)			
(27,996)			

FA Cup goalscorer: Chivers

Football League Cup

Date	Opponent		Score
Sep 11	Middlesbrough	(h)	0-4
(Round 2)			
(15,216)			

1975-6

After missing relegation by the skin of their teeth following a bad start to the previous season, Tottenham Hotspur approached 1975-6 with a good deal of apprehension. They knew that only a point separated them from lining up with the Second Division clubs for the new campaign. But a Steve Perryman goal on the opening day was enough to give Tottenham their first points when Middlesbrough came to White Hart Lane and went down 1-0. The match was also full-back Joe Kinnear's last for Spurs. Twelve days later the Eire international who had played almost 200 League games for the club moved to the South coast and Brighton and Hove Albion.

John Duncan, who joined Spurs the previous season and became top scorer with twelve goals, was on target when Ipswich came to White Hart Lane for the second match, a 1-1 draw, and when Liverpool beat them 3-2 in their first away match, it looked as though Tottenham fans were doomed for another season of suspense and agony as their side battled against the drop. But after a 3-2 home defeat by Derby County sent them into a relegation spot of twentieth place on 13 September, Spurs began to climb slowly up the table, and by the beginning of December they were in thirteenth place. Duncan had scored two goals in a game in consecutive matches as Tottenham beat Burnley and Sheffield United, 2-1 apiece.

The second half of the season belonged in many ways to Spurs. After losing 3-1 at home to Birmingham on Boxing Day 1975, Spurs were beaten only five times in their remaining nineteen games and a 2-0 win over Arsenal on 3 April saw them rocket up to sixth place in the First Division. Eventually the Tottenham club managed a creditable ninth place — not bad for a side which had narrowly missed relegation twelve months earlier.

In the FA Cup Tottenham fared less well, going out in the third round to unfancied Stoke City. At White Hart Lane, Spurs could only draw 1-1 with the Potteries club and when they met at the Victoria Ground, Moores and Salmon (penalty) sent Stoke through.

It was the Football League Cup which offered Spurs a chance of Wembley in 1975-6. Chris Jones scored the goal which beat Watford in the second round and John Pratt and Alfie Conn removed Crewe Alexandra 2-0 — a far cry from the day when Spurs beat the Cheshire club 13-2 in the FA Cup.

Nearly 50,000 fans packed White Hart Lane to see Spurs and West Ham United fight out a goalless draw in the fourth round. At Upton Park there were still no goals in the ninety minutes of ordinary time but when the tie went into extra-time, John Duncan and Willie Young were on hand to snap up the chances that sent Spurs forward to an easy fifth round tie with Doncaster Rovers. Poor Doncaster! They ran into Spurs at their best and John Duncan crashed home a hat-trick to send them well on the way to a 7-2 win. Martin Chivers scored twice, John Pratt once, and even Doncaster's Les Chappell got on the Spurs scoresheet with an unfortunate own goal.

Alfie Conn and Joe Kinnear in happier days, Kinnear played only one game for Spurs in 1975-6 and Conn's White Hart Lane career was also on a downward trail.

Spurs were through to yet another Football League Cup semi-final but there it was to end. John Pratt scored to give Spurs a slender 1-0 lead in the first-leg against Newcastle United at White Hart Lane but that was never enough to take to St James's Park. Although Don McAllister found the back of United's net, goals by Gowling, Keeley and Nulty before 51,000 roaring Newcastle fans, saw the Magpies into the Football League Cup Final, where they lost to Manchester City at Wembley. For Tottenham there was only First Division survival to play for now. They achieved it with comparative ease.

First Division results 1975-6

Aug 16   Middlesbrough   (h)   1-0
(Perryman   25,502)

Aug 20   Ipswich Town   (h)   1-1
(Duncan   28,311)

Aug 23   Liverpool   (a)   2-3
(Duncan, Jones   42,729)

Aug 25   West Ham Utd   (a)   0-1
(35,914)

Aug 30   Norwich City   (h)   2-2
(Pratt, Duncan   23,145)

Sep 6   Manchester Utd   (a)   2-3
(Jones, Chivers   51,641)

Sep 13   Derby County   (h)   2-3
(Duncan, Chivers   28,455)

Sep 20   Leeds Utd   (a)   1-1
(Pratt   27,372)

Sep 27   Arsenal   (h)   0-0
(37,092)

Oct 4   Newcastle Utd   (a)   2-2
(Pratt, Duncan   32,235)

Oct 11   Aston Villa   (a)   1-1
(Pratt   40,048)

Oct 18   Manchester City   (h)   2-2
(Jones 2   30,502)

Oct 25   Leicester C   (a)   3-2
(Coates, Chivers, Perryman   22,088)

Nov 1   Wolves   (h)   2-1
(Neighbour, Young   26,102)

Nov 8   QPR   (a)   0-0
(28,454)

Nov 15   Stoke City   (h)   1-1
(Jones   25,698)

Nov 22   Manchester C   (a)   1-2
(Osgood   31,456)

Nov 29   Burnley   (h)   2-1
(Duncan 2   21,222)

Dec 6   Sheffield Utd   (a)   2-1
(Duncan 2   23,909)

Dec 10   Everton   (h)   2-2
(Pratt, Duncan   18,638)

Dec 13   Liverpool   (h)   0-4
(29,891)

Dec 20   Middlesbrough   (a)   0-1
(22,000)

Dec 26   Birmingham C   (h)   1-3
(Chivers pen   21,651)

Dec 27   Coventry C   (a)   2-2
(Duncan 2   21,094)

Jan 10   Derby County   (a)   3-2
(Neighbour, Perryman, McAllister   28,085)

Jan 17   Manchester U   (h)   1-1
(Duncan   49,387)

Jan 31   Ipswich Town   (a)   2-1
(Coates, Osgood pen   24,072)

Feb 7   West Ham Utd   (h)   1-1
(Duncan   32,832)

Feb 14   QPR   (h)   0-3
(28,,200)

Feb 21   Stoke City   (a)   2-1
(Duncan, Hoddle,   17,113)

Feb 24   Everton   (a)   0-1
(18,126)

Feb 28   Leicester City   (h)   1-1
(Chivers   21,427)

Mar 6   Norwich City   (a)   1-3
(Chivers   21,220)

Mar 13   Aston Villa   (h)   5-2
(Nicholl   own   goal,   Perryman,   Duncan,
McAllister, Robinson   23,169)

Mar 16   Wolves   (a)   1-0
(Pratt   21,544)

Mar 20   Burnley   (a)   2-1
(Duncan, Pratt   15,465)

Mar 27   Sheffield Utd   (h)   5-0
(Young, Duncan, Perryman 2, Chivers 21,370)

Apr 3   Arsenal   (a)   2-0
(Pratt, Duncan   42,134)

Apr 10   Leeds United   (h)   0-0
(40,359)

Apr 17   Birmingham C   (a)   1-3
(Pratt   30,616)

Apr 19   Coventry C   (h)   4-1
(Osgood, Neighbour, Pratt, Duncan   21,107)

Apr 24   Newcastle Utd   (h)   0-3
(30,049)

Final League Record
P42, W14, D15, L13, F63, A63, Pts 43,
Pos 9th
League goalscorers: Duncan 20, Pratt 10,
Chivers 7, Perryman 6, Jones 5, Neighbour 3,
Osgood 3, Coates 2, McAllister 2, Young 2,
Hoddle 1, Robinson 1, own goal 1

FA Cup
Jan 3   Stoke City   (h)   1-1
(Round 3)
(Duncan   26,715)
Jan 24   Stoke City   (a)   1-2
(replay)
(Perryman   29,538)
FA Cup goalscorers: Duncan, Perryman

Football League Cup

Sep 9   Watford   (a)   1-0
(Round 2)
(Jones 14,997)
Oct 8   Crewe Alex   (a)   2-0
(Round 3)
(Pratt, Conn 10,500)
 Nov 12 West Ham Utd   (h)   0-0
(Round 4)
(49,125)
Nov 24 West Ham Utd   (a)   2-0
(replay)
(Duncan, Young 38,443) after extra time
Dec 3   Doncaster   (h)   7-2

(Round 5)
(Duncan 3, Pratt, Chappell own goal, Chivers
2 25,702)
Jan 14 Newcastle U   (h)   1-0
(SF 1st leg)
(Pratt 40,215)
Jan 21 Newcastle U   (a)   1-3
(SF 2nd leg)
(McAllister 51,000)
Spurs lost 2-3 on aggregate

Football League Cup goalscorers:
Duncan 4, Pratt 3, Chivers 2, Conn 1, Jones 1,
Young 1, McAllister 1, own goal 1

*Chris Jones finds a way through Coventry City
defenders Jim Holmes and Mick Coop.*

1976-7

After narrowly missing relegation to the Second Division in 1974-5, Tottenham Hotspur enjoyed something of a reprieve the following season when they climbed to an unexpected ninth in the First Division, as well as reaching the semi-finals of the League Cup. But it was only a temporary stay of execution and in 1976-7, Spurs slumped to bottom place in the table and the bitter prospect of relegation.

All season Spurs hovered round the relegation zone and from an opening day defeat by Ipswich Town at Portman Road, it was obvious that the White Hart Lane club would be sampling Second Division football in the immediate future. Yet Tottenham's first win of the season — on 4 September when they were eighteenth in the table —

proved to be one of their most epic victories. Before 60,000 Manchester United fans at Old Trafford, Ralph Coates, John Pratt and Ian Moores gave Tottenham a 3-2 win to hoist them up four places in the table.

Spurs' troubles had started as early as 23 June when manager Terry Neill resigned and shortly afterwards, moved across North London to become manager of Spurs' old enemies, Arsenal. On 1 July, Martin Chivers signed for the Swiss side Servette Geneva for £80,000 and the Tottenham outfit of the mid-Seventies was breaking up. Fourteen days into July and coach Keith Burkinshaw was promoted to

Pat Jennings in action. Spurs fans were stunned when they realised that 1976-7 was the Irish international's last season at White Hart Lane.

Don McAllister scored Spurs second goal in the 3-3 draw with Everton at White Hart Lane in October 1976. Dai Davies is the unfortunate Everton goalkeeper.

take Neill's job, and by the end of his first month in charge, Burkinshaw had set up the transfer of David Johnson from Ipswich Town — only to hear Johnson decline to join Tottenham. Burkinshaw's first move in the transfer market came on 30 September when Peter Taylor came to White Hart Lane from fellow-Londoners Crystal Palace for £200,000. On the same day, Jimmy Neighbour went the other way and he signed for Norwich City for £75,000.

But Burkinshaw had an unenviable task in front of him and even the return of Bill Nicholson as adviser could do nothing to arrest the downward path that Spurs were treading. By Christmas, they were twentieth in the table and had been humiliatingly knocked out of the Football League Cup by Third Division Wrexham. At White Hart Lane on 22 September, before less than 20,000 fans, Spurs went down 3-2 when they were hit by goals from Mike Thomas (2) and Bill Ashcroft.

The New Year held little cheer for Spurs fans and when the third round of the FA Cup came round on 8 January, Cardiff's Welsh international Peter Sayer scored the only goal of the game at Ninian

Park and Spurs were left with nothing to look forward to but First Division survival. Tottenham Hotspur failed and failed miserably. The second half of the season was a nightmare for them. In their last twenty-one games, Spurs won only seven and lost ten matches. The rare victories were over Ipswich, Norwich, Birmingham, Leicester, Aston Villa, QPR, and, surprisingly, Liverpool.

Tottenham had used twenty-two players in a forlorn bid to stay in the First Division and only Keith Osgood and Steve Perryman had played in every league match. During the season, on 1 March 1977, Alfie Conn had joined Celtic for £60,000, although he had to serve a one-month probation to establish his fitness.

Burkinshaw had juggled around the players at his disposal without effect, although it must be said that the newly-promoted coach faced an uphill struggle with a Spurs side which might well have seen Second Division football a couple of seasons earlier. Nevertheless, Burkinshaw was already formulating a plan to make a speedy return to the top flight and Spurs sojourn in the Second Division was to be as brief as possible.

First Division results 1976-7

Aug 21   Ipswich Town   (a)   1-3
(Jones 28,859)

Aug 25   Newcastle U   (h)   0-2
(24,002)

Aug 28   Middlesbrough   (h)   0-0
(21,720)

Sep 4   Man United   (a)   3-2
(Coates, Moores, Pratt 60,743)

Sep 11   Leeds United   (h)   1-0
(Jones 35,525)

Sep 18   Liverpool   (a)   0-2
(47,421)

Sep 25   Norwich City   (h)   1-1
(Hoddle 27,440)

Oct 2   West Brom   (a)   2-4
(Jones, Taylor 23,495)

Oct 16   Derby County   (a)   2-8
(Perryman, Osgood pen 24,216)

Oct 20   Birmingham C   (h)   1-0
(Osgood pen, 20,193)

Oct 23   Coventry City   (h)   0-1
(21,877)

Oct 30   Everton   (h)   3-3
(Pratt, McAllister, Osgood pen 26,027)

Nov 6   West Ham Utd   (a)   3-5
(Duncan, Hoddle, Osgood pen 28,997)

Nov 13   Bristol City   (h)   0-1
(28,795)

Nov 20   Sunderland   (a)   1-2
(Moores 30,324)

Nov 27   Stoke City   (h)   2-0
(Osgood 2 (1 pen) 22,230)

Dec 11   Man City   (h)   2-2
(Taylor 2 24,608)

Dec 18   Leicester C   (a)   1-2
(Coates 16,397)

Dec 27   Arsenal   (h)   2-2
(Young, Duncan 47,751)

Jan 1   West Ham Utd   (h)   2-1
(Osgood pen, Duncan 44,972)

Jan 11   QPR   (a)   1-2
(Duncan 24,266)

Jan 22   Ipswich Town   (h)   1-0
(Taylor 35,126)

Feb 5   Middlesbrough   (a)   0-2
(21,000)

Feb 12   Man United   (h)   1-3
(Jones 46.946)

Feb 19   Leeds United   (a)   1-2
(Armstrong 26,858)

Feb 26   Newcastle Utd   (a)   0-2
(29,401)

Mar 5   Norwich City   (a)   3-1
(Taylor, Pratt, Armstrong, 23,554)

Mar 9   Liverpool   (h)   1-0
(Coates 32,098)

Mar 12   West Brom   (h)   0-2
(28,834)

Mar 19   Birmingham C   (a)   2-1
(Hoddle, Jones 23,398)

Mar 23   Derby County   (h)   0-0
(27,359)

Mar 26   Everton   (a)   0-4
(32,549)

Apr 2   Coventry City   (a)   1-1
(Taylor 16,275)

Apr 9   QPR   (h)   3-0
(Taylor, Jones 2 32,680)

Apr 11   Arsenal   (a)   0-1
(47,296)

Apr 12   Bristol City   (a)   0-1
(28,101)

Apr 16   Sunderland   (h)   1-1
(Jones 34,185)

Apr 20   Aston Villa   (a)   1-2
(Armstrong 42,047)

Apr 23   Stoke City   (a)   0-0
(15,641)

Apr 30   Aston Villa   (h)   3-1
(Hoddle, Jones, Taylor 30,890)

May 7   Man City   (a)   0-5
(37,919)

May 14   Leicester City   (h)   2-0
(Holmes, Pratt 26,094)

Final League Record
P42, W12, D9, L21, F48, A72, Pts 33,
Pos 22nd

Football League goalscorers:
Jones 9, Taylor 8, Osgood 7, Pratt 4, Hoddle 4, Duncan 4, Armstrong 3, Coates 3, Moores 2, Perryman 1, Young 1, Holmes 1, McAllister 1

FA Cup
Jan 8   Cardiff City   (a)   0-1
(Round 3)
(27,868)

Football League Cup
Aug 31   Middlesbrough   (a)   2-1
(Round 2)
(Moores, Neighbour 19,000)

Sep 22   Wrexham   (h)   2-3
(Round 3)
(Hoddle, Moores 19,156)

Football League Cup goalscorers: Moores 2, Hoddle, Neighbour

1977-8

Tottenham Hotspur bounced straight back to the First Division after spending just one season in the Second in 1977-8. But they gave their supporters a nail-biting end to the season with the issue not decided until the very last match — and then only by the narrowest of margins.

Nine days before the start of the season, Spurs fans were stunned at the news that long-serving goalkeeper Pat Jennings — still considered one of the best in the world — was ending a thirteen-year association with Spurs. And to add insult to injury for Tottenham fans, Jennings was moving just three miles across North London to begin a new career with Spurs arch-rivals, Arsenal. One man who was not leaving White Hart Lane, however, was winger Peter Taylor. Manager Keith Burkinshaw turned down an offer from West German club St Pauli of Hamburg.

Spurs season started off in fine style when they beat Sheffield United 4-2 at White Hart Lane in the opening match, and then earned an away point at Blackburn. Spurs went on like this for the first eight games, during which time they picked up thirteen points to head the Second Division table by the beginning of October, while an easy 4-0 win over Wimbledon in the Football League Cup put Spurs through to the third round.

On 20 October, Tottenham paid Torquay United £60,000 for twenty-one-year-old striker Colin Lee — a record fee for the Devon club — and two days later, Lee made a sensational debut for Spurs. Bristol Rovers visited White Hart Lane and provided the opposition for Spurs biggest-ever League win. The scoreline was an astonishing 9-0 and Lee scored four of them! Also in hat-trick form was Ian Moores and Hoddle and Taylor added the others.

The following Wednesday evening, however, Spurs delight turned to disappointment as they faced Coventry City in the third round of the League Cup. City won 3-2 and Tottenham could now turn their attentions solely to the business of getting out of the Second Division — until January and FA Cup time, at least.

Spurs made good use of the time between their League Cup exit and the third round of the FA Cup. In twelve matches they earned seventeen points and were beaten just once — by Bolton Wanderers at Burnden Park at the end of November. On New Years Day 1978, Spurs were second in the table and heading for a rapid return to the top flight.

It was Bolton who ended Spurs interest in the 1977-8 FA Cup, almost before it had begun. After a 2-2 draw at White Hart Lane in their third round

Glen Hoddle scored some vital goals as Spurs bounced straight back to the First Division.

clash, the two clubs met again in Lancashire and although the game went to extra time, it was Bolton who took final advantage of their home game and won 2-1. Unfettered by outside interests, Tottenham Hotspur put down their heads and marched towards the First Division.

A 2-1 win at home to Cardiff on 21 January sent them back to the top of the Second Division where they stayed until the middle of April with a run of fourteen matches, six wins and six draws. But the points lost in those draws looked like costing Tottenham dearly. And when Burnley beat them 2-1—and then their closest rivals Brighton took both points in a 3-1 win—it seemed that perhaps Spurs would miss out at the very last hurdle. The Brighton defeat was followed by one against Sunderland and only a hotly-disputed goal by Perryman earned Spurs a 1-0 win over Hull. The final match clinched it. A goalless draw at Southampton saw First Division football back at Tottenham—although in the end they made it only on goal difference from Brighton.

Terry Naylor (white shirt) completed his 200th League game for Spurs in this promotion season.

Second Division results 1977-8

Aug 20 Sheffield Utd (h) 4-2
(Duncan, Jones, Osgood 2 pens 27,673)
Aug 24 Blackburn R (a) 0-0
(9,540)
Aug 27 Notts County (h) 2-1
(Duncan 2 25,839)
Sep 3 Cardiff City (a) 0-0
(8,901)
Sep 10 Fulham (h) 1-0
(Jones 31,939)
Sep 17 Blackpool (a) 2-0
(Hoddle, Duncan 17,077)
Sep 24 Luton Town (h) 2-0
(Osgood pen, Jones 32,814)
Oct 1 Orient (a) 1-1
(Taylor 24,131)
Oct 4 Hull City (a) 0-2
(10,966)
Oct 8 Oldham Athletic (h) 5-1
(Duncan 2, Robinson, Taylor 2 24,636)
Oct 15 Charlton Ath (a) 1-4
(Taylor 30,706)
Oct 22 Bristol Rov (h) 9-0
(Lee 4, Taylor, Moores 3, Hoddle 26,311)
Oct 29 Stoke City (a) 3-1
(Armstrong 2, Pratt 21,012)
Nov 5 Burnley (h) 3-0
(Taylor, McNab, Hoddle 30,634)
Nov 12 Crystal Palace (a) 2-1
(Moores, Duncan 40,277)
Nov 19 Brighton (h) 0-0
(48,613)
Nov 26 Bolton Wand (a) 0-1
(32,266)
Dec 3 Southampton (h) 0-0
(37,873)
Dec 10 Sunderland (a) 2-1
(Duncan 2 31,960)
Dec 17 Crystal Palace (h) 2-2
(Hoddle 2 33,211)
Dec 26 Millwall (a) 3-1
(Taylor, Lee, Duncan 15,036)
Dec 27 Mansfield T (h) 1-1
(Duncan 36,288)
Dec 31 Blackburn R (h) 4-0
(Hoddle, Pratt, Lee 2 30,520)
Jan 2 Sheffield Utd (a) 2-2
(Duncan, Taylor 31,207)
Jan 14 Notts County (a) 3-3
(Lee, Pratt 2 15,709)
Jan 21 Cardiff City (h) 2-1
(Duncan 2 29,104)
Feb 4 Fulham (a) 1-1
(Taylor 24,758)
Feb 11 Blackpool (h) 2-2
(Pratt, McAllister 28,707)

Feb 22 Luton Town (a) 4-1
(Hoddle 2, McAllister, Duncan 17,024)
Feb 25 Orient (h) 1-1
(Lee 32,869)
Mar 4 Oldham Ath (a) 1-1
(McNab 14,118)
Mar 11 Charlton Ath (h) 2-1
(Hoddle pen, Pratt 34,511)
Mar 18 Bristol Rov (a) 3-2
(Jones, McNab, Pratt 17,708)
Mar 22 Stoke City (h) 3-1
(McAllister, Lee 2 30,646)
Mar 25 Mansfield T (a) 3-3
(Jones, Hoddle 2 (1 pen) 12,106)
Mar 27 Millwall (h) 3-3
(Jones 2, Hoddle 33,074)
Apr 1 Burnley (a) 1-2
(Taylor 16,790)
Apr 8 Bolton Wand (h) 1-0
(McAllister 50,097)
Apr 15 Brighton (a) 1-3
(Jones 32,647)
Apr 22 Sunderland (h) 2-3
(Taylor, Duncan 38,220)
Apr 26 Hull City (h) 1-0
(Perryman 36,913)
Apr 29 Southampton (a) 0-0
(28,846)

Final League Record
P42, W20, D16, L6, F73, A49, Pts 56,
Pos 3rd

Football League goalscorers: Duncan 16,
Hoddle 12, Lee 11, Taylor 11, Jones 8, Pratt
7, McAllister 4, Moores 4, McNab 3, Osgood
3, Armstrong 2, Perryman 1, Robinson 1

FA Cup
Jan 7 Bolton Wand (h) 2-2
(Round 3)
(Duncan, Hoddle 43,731)
Jan 10 Bolton Wand (a) 1-2
(replay)
(Taylor pen 31,314) after extra time
FA Cup goalscorers: Duncan, Hoddle Taylor

Football League Cup
Aug 31 Wimbledon (h) 4-0
(Round 2)
(Duncan 3, Osgood pen 22,807)
Oct 26 Coventry C (h) 2-3
(Round 3)
(Pratt, Armstrong 35,199)

Football League Cup goalscorers: Duncan 3,
Pratt, Armstrong, Osgood

1978-9

For Tottenham Hotspur fans the 1978-9 season began on 10 July — the day they awoke to find that Spurs had caused a sensation by signing Argentinian World Cup stars, Osvaldo Ardiles and Ricardo Villa for a combined fee of £700,000 — Ardiles from Hurican and Villa from Racing Club. Manager Keith Burkinshaw told an excited Press conference: 'This proves we think big — we want to be one of the best clubs in the country.' England winger Peter Taylor added: 'This is magical news. Ardiles and Villa will pack grounds wherever they play.' The players' union was not so sure. The PFA's Gordon Taylor criticised Tottenham: 'What Spurs have done is to put two English footballers out of work.'

But whatever people thought, Villa and Ardiles made their debuts in a 3-1 win over Antwerp on the club's pre-season tour. Later in the same tour, another controversial signing, centre-half John Lacy, was sent off in a friendly match against Velno in Holland. Lacy was one of the first players to go to the Independent Tribunal after Fulham valued him £50,000 higher than Spurs' valuation. At length, Spurs had their bargain.

But it was Villa and Ardiles who everyone wanted to see. In the opening League match at Nottingham Forest over 41,000 packed the City Ground and saw Villa make an immediate impact by scoring the equaliser which took a point from the

Spurs v Everton at White Hart Lane in May 1979. This furious action around the Spurs goal ended in a goal kick.

First Division results 1978-9

Aug 19 Nottm Forest (a) 1-1
(Villa 41,223)

Aug 23 Aston Villa (h) 1-4
(Hoddle pen, 47,892)

Aug 26 Chelsea (h) 2-2
(Duncan, Armstrong 40,632)

Sep 2 Liverpool (a) 0-7
(50,705)

Sep 9 Bristol C (h) 1-0
(Rodgers own goal 34,035)

Sep 16 Leeds Utd (a) 2-1
(Taylor, Lee 36,062)

Sep 23 Man City (a) 0-2
(43,471)

Sep 30 Coventry C (h) 1-1
(Hoddle 35,006)

Oct 7 West Brom (a) 1-0
(Taylor 33,211)

Oct 14 Birmingham C (h) 1-0
(Ainscow own goal 41,230)

Oct 21 Derby County (a) 2-2
(Taylor, McAllister 26,181)

Oct 28 Bolton W (h) 2-0
(Lee, Pratt 37,337)

Nov 4 Norwich City (a) 2-2
(Lee, Taylor 25,695)

Nov 11 Nottm Forest (h) 1-3
(Pratt 50,541)

Nov 18 Chelsea (a) 3-1
(Lee 2, Hoddle 41,594)

Nov 22 Liverpool (h) 0-0
(50,393)

Nov 25 Wolves (h) 1-0
(Taylor 35,450)

Dec 9 Ipswich (h) 1-0
(Pratt 33,882)

Dec 16 Man Utd (a) 0-2
(52,026)

Dec 23 Arsenal (h) 0-5
(42,273)

Dec 26 QPR (a) 2-2
(Lee, Taylor pen 24,845)

Dec 30 Everton (a) 1-1
(Lee 44,363)

Jan 13 Bristol C (a) 0-0
(28,781)

Jan 20 Leeds Utd (h) 1-2
(Hoddle 36,828)

Feb 3 Man City (h) 0-3
(32,037)

Feb 10 Coventry C (a) 3-1
(Taylor 2, Lee 25,133)

Feb 24 Birmingham C (a) 0-1
(20,980)

Mar 3 Derby County (h) 2-0
(Ardiles 2 28,089)

Mar 17 Norwich City (h) 0-0
(24,982)

Mar 24 Aston Villa (a) 3-2

(Hoddle 2, Jones 35,486)

Mar 28 Southampton (h) 0-0
(23,570)

Mar 31 Middlesbrough (a) 0-1
(19,172)

Apr 3 Wolves (a) 2-3
(Jones 2 19,819)

Apr 7 Middlesbrough (h) 1-2
(Taylor pen 21,580)

Apr 10 Arsenal (a) 0-1
(54,041)

Apr 14 QPR (h) 1-1
(Perryman 28,853)

Apr 16 Southampton (a) 3-3
(Taylor, Jones, Pratt 22,096)

Apr 21 Man Utd (h) 1-1
(Jones 36,665)

Apr 28 Ipswich (a) 1-2
(Hoddle pen 28,179)

May 5 Everton (h) 1-1
(Ardiles 26,077)

May 8 Bolton W (a) 3-1
(Falco, Alardyce own goal, Holmes; 17,879)

May 14 West Brom (h) 1-0
(Villa 24,789)

Final League Record

P42, W13, D15, L14, F48, A61, Pts 41,
Pos 11th

League goalscorers: Taylor 10, Lee 8, Hoddle
7, Jones 5, Pratt 4, Ardiles 3, Villa 2, Duncan
1, Armstrong 1, McAllister 1, Perryman 1,
Falco 1, Holmes 1, own goals 3

Football League Cup

Aug 29 Swansea City (a) 2-2
(Round 2)
(Hoddle, Armstrong 24,335)

Sep 6 Swansea City (h) 1-3
(replay)
(Villa 33,672)

Football League Cup goalscorers: Armstrong,
Hoddle, Villa

FA Cup

Jan 10   Altrincham   (h)   1-1
(Round 3)
(Taylor pen   31,081)
Jan 16   Altrincham   (a)   3-0
(replay)
(Lee 3   27,878)
Feb 12   Wrexham   (h)   3-3
(Round 4)
(Roberts own goal, Hoddle, Jones   27,120)
Feb 21   Wrexham   (a)   3-2
(replay)
(Jones 3   16,050)

Feb 28   Oldham Ath   (a)   1-0
(Round 5)
(Perryman   16,097)
Mar 10   Man Utd   (h)   1-1
(Round 6)
(Ardiles   51,800)
Mar 14   Man Utd   (a)   0-2
(replay)
(54,510)

FA Cup goalscorers: Jones 4, Lee 3, Taylor 1, Hoddle 1, Perryman 1, Ardiles 1, own goal 1

reigning champions. Four days later, White Hart Lane looked more like Buenos Aires as 47,000 ecstatic Spurs fans gave Ardiles and Villa a World-Cup-style ticker-tape welcome on their home debuts. Aston Villa refused to join in the celebrations and went 1-0 up at half-time. In the second half Villa (Aston, not Ricardo!) scored three more goals and Spurs had only a Glen Hoddle penalty to show for all the razmatazz.

The Argentinians became marked men. In the second round of the League Cup at Swansea in late August, a crunching tackle by former Liverpool strongman Tommy Smith put Ardiles out of the match and Spurs were lucky to escape with a 2-2 draw. In the replay, Villa scored to show that the Argentinians could not be intimidated, but Toshack and Charles had already put Swansea 2-0 ahead and when Curtis added a third, Spurs became the first giantkilling victims of the new season. On 14 October, Ardiles and Villa met up with their Argentinian team mate Alberto Tarantini when they beat Birmingham City 1-0 to move up to sixth place — six weeks before, Spurs had gone spinning to their heaviest-ever defeat when Liverpool beat them 7-0 to send them to 21st place in the First Division.

Spurs real hope of success was in the FA Cup — although twice they threatened to repeat the shock Cup exit at the hands of Swansea. When Northern Premier League club Altrincham Town drew Spurs away in the third round of the FA Cup, few people gave a second thought to the possibility of an upset. But when Geoff Johnson equalised Peter Taylor's penalty in the dying minutes, there were some red faces. The Cheshire club opted for cash not glory and the replay was at Maine Road where Colin Lee's hat-trick put the form book straight with a 3-0 win. In the fourth round Spurs almost floundered again when it took all their skill and experience to hold Wrexham 3-3 in London. In Wales it was Chris Jones with the second Spurs hat-trick in consecutive replays who put them through 3-2. Oldham fell 1-0 in the fifth round before Spurs interest in the season came to an end. Ardiles sixth

John Lacy (No 5) heads clear a Manchester United attack during the League game at White Hart Lane in April 1979. United's Gordon McIlroy looks on.

round header against Manchester United was equalised by Micky Thomas and in the Old Trafford replay Sammy McIlroy put the final nail in Spurs coffin.

1979-80

Tottenham Hotspur's season began and ended in anti-climax. But sandwiched in between the first-day win by Middlesbrough at White Hart Lane and the last-day draw at home to relegated Bristol City, was an FA Cup run which for a time looked as though it might take Spurs all the way to Wembley

With Liverpool dominating the First Division championship — though a 2-0 win by Spurs at Anfield late in the season meant that the eventual runners-up Manchester United had fresh, if brief, hope — Tottenham Hotspur had to look to one of the two domestic knockout competitions for success. In the first such competition to come along — the Football League Cup — Spurs went out at the first hurdle after they could only take a one goal advantage to Old Trafford after the first-leg and where United made short work of advancing to the next stage.

But the FA Cup was a different story. The third round draw paired Spurs with United yet again. And when they could only draw 1-1 at White Hart Lane, the writing appeared to be on the wall for Tottenham. The White Hart Lane tie was full of incident and controversy. Referee Pat Partridge turned down four appeals for Spurs penalties — though at least two were more in hope than in anger — and then awarded United a lifeline when a penalty to the Red Devils of Old Trafford negated Osvaldo Ardiles earlier goal and sent the whole show back to Manchester. But Spurs were not to be outdone a second time — even though they lost goalkeeper Milija Aleksic with an injury — and with Hoddle taking over in goal, over 53,000 fans saw Spurs hang on to another Ardiles goal.

Swindon proved a more difficult proposition in the fourth round and Spurs only removed them

Spurs playing staff 1979-80: Back row (left to right): McAllister, Hoddle, Villa, Kendall, Lacy, Lee, Daines, Falco, Armstrong, Naylor. Middle row: Varney (physiotherapist), Chambers, Jones, Galvin, O'Reilly, Aleksic, Miller, Mazzon, Brooke, Wallis (trainer), Welton (assistant manager). Front row: Dickenson, Ardiles, Beavon, Smith, Perryman (captain), Burkinshaw (manager), Mr S. A. Wale (chairman), Pratt, Holmes, Grayling, Hazard, Emms.
Apprentices: Bolton, Crook, Southey, Corbett, Hamill, Parks, Cooper, Harvey, Gibson.

First Division results 1979-80

Aug 18   Middlesbrough   (h)   1-3
(Hoddle   32,743)
Aug 22   Norwich   (a)   0-4
(17,670)
Aug 25   Stoke City   (a)   1-3
(Perryman   22,832)
Sep 1   Man City   (h)   2-1
(Hoddle, Jones   30,901)
Sep 8   Brighton   (h)   2-1
(Armstrong, Hoddle   34,107)
Sep 15   Southampton   (a)   2-5
(Hoddle, Jones   22,573)
Sep 22   West Brom   (h)   1-1
(Hoddle   29,814)
Sep 29   Coventry   (a)   1-1
(Jones   20,125)
Oct 6   Crystal Palace   (a)   1-1
(Villa   45,296)
Oct 10   Norwich   (h)   3-2
(Hoddle 2, Villa   26,488)
Oct 13   Derby   (h)   1-0
(Armstrong   33,269)
Oct 20   Leeds   (a)   2-1
(Armstrong, Jones   25,203)
Oct 27   Nottm Forest   (h)   1-0
(Hoddle   49,038)
Nov 3   Middlesbrough   (a)   0-0
(20,079)
Nov 10   Bolton   (h)   2-0
(Yorath, Hoddle   33,155)
Nov 17   Liverpool   (a)   1-2
(Jones   51,092)
Nov 24   Everton   (a)   1-1
(Jones   31,071)
Dec 1   Man United   (h)   1-2
(Hoddle   51,389)
Dec 8   Bristol City   (a)   3-1
(Miller, Hoddle 2   25,093)
Dec 15   Aston Villa   (h)   1-2
(Ardiles   30,555)
Dec 21   Ipswich   (a)   1-3
(McAllister   18,852)
Dec 26   Arsenal   (a)   0-1
(48,357)
Dec 29   Stoke   (h)   1-0
(Pratt   28,810)
Jan 12   Man City   (a)   1-1
(Hoddle   34,837)
Jan 19   Brighton   (a)   2-0
(Hughton, Villa   29,417)
Feb 2   Southampton   (h)   0-0
(37,155)

Feb 9   West Brom   (a)   1-2
(Hoddle   26,320)
Feb 23   Derby   (a)   1-2
(Galvin   21,183)
Feb 27   Coventry   (h)   4-3
(Hoddle 3, Falco   22,536)
Mar 1   Leeds   (h)   2-1
(Hoddle, Falco   35,331)
Mar 11   Nottm Forest   (a)   0-4
(25,633)
Mar 15   Crystal Palace   (h)   0-0
(28,419)
Mar 22   Bolton   (a)   1-2
(Jones   14,474)
Mar 29   Liverpool   (a)   2-0
(Hoddle, Pratt   32,114)
Apr 2   Ipswich   (h)   0-2
(26,423)
Apr 5   Wolves   (h)   2-1
(Jones, Galvin   30,713)
Apr 7   Arsenal   (h)   1-2
(Jones   41,365)
Apr 12   Man United   (a)   1-4
(Ardiles   53,151)
Apr 19   Everton   (h)   3-0
(Miller, Ardiles, Galvin   25,245)
Apr 23   Wolves   (h)   2-2
(Armstrong, Galvin   19,843)
Apr 26   Aston Villa   (a)   0-1
(29,549)
May 3   Bristol City   (h)   0-0
(23,585)

Final League Record
P42, W15, D10, L17, F52, A62, Pts 40,
Pos 14th

League goalscorers: Hoddle 19, Jones 9, Armstrong 4, Galvin 4, Villa 3, Ardiles 3, Miller 2, Pratt 2, Falco 2, Hughton 1, McAllister 1, Yorath 1, Perryman 1

Football League Cup
Aug 29   Man United   (h)   2-1
(Rd 2 1st leg)
(Pratt, Hoddle   29,163)
Sep 5   Man United   (a)   1-3
(Rd 2 2nd leg)
(Armstrong   48,292)
Football League Cup goalscorers: Pratt, Hoddle, Armstrong

FA Cup

Jan 5	Man United	(h)	1-1
(Round 3)			
(Ardiles 45,207)			
Jan 9	Man United	(a)	1-0
(replay)			
(Ardiles 53,762)			
Jan 26	Swindon	(a)	0-0
(Round 4)			
(26,000)			
Jan 30	Swindon	(h)	2-1
(replay)			
(Armstrong 2 46,707)			
Feb 16	Birmingham	(h)	3-1
(Round 5)			
(Armstrong, Hoddle 2 49,936)			
Mar 8	Liverpool	(h)	0-1
(Round 6)			
(48,033)			

FA Cup goalscorers: Armstrong 3, Ardiles 2, Hoddle 2

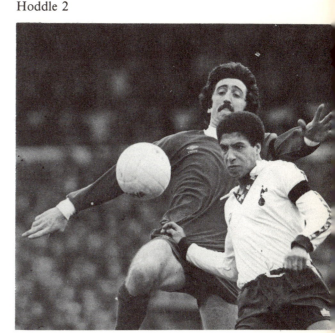

Christ Hughton was one of the young players who made a mark at White Hart Lane in 1979-80. Here he tangles with Liverpool's David Johnson as Spurs win 2-0 to cause a flutter at the top of the First Division.

after a goalless draw in Wiltshire. Then Birmingham City fell 3-1 at White Hart Lane and Tottenham fans weighed up the prospect of a visit from Liverpool for the quarter-finals. But arrangements for a possible trip to Wembley had to be hastily cancelled. Terry McDermott scored the only goal — and what a brilliant goal it was too — and then Liverpool sewed up the middle of the field and never allowed the Londoners chance to break back into the game. Spurs Wembley dreams were over for another year but as Burkinshaw said afterwards: 'We learned a lot this afternoon and I think that we can prove ourselves to be like Liverpool — and that can be no bad thing!'

So Tottenham's season was effectively over and the First Division table, where they finished an uninspiring 14th, did little to console their fans.

And yet 1979-80 was a significant season at White Hart Lane with young players like Chris Hughton, Mark Falco, Paul Miller and Terry Gibson coming through to the First Division stage. Veteran skipper Steve Perryman, the veteran of over 400 League games and the winner of cup medals with Tottenham since he made his debut in September 1969 as an 18-year-old, has plans to lead Spurs to further glory before he hangs up his boots.

Spurs season finally ended with news of a super stadium at White Hart Lane for the 'eighties. A £3 million West Stand seating 7,000 spectators and housing seventy-two private boxes is the first stage of a plan to make the ground an all-seater stadium. It is all a far cry from the days of gas lights and those first Spurs matches on the Tottenham Marshes!

TWELVE GREAT SPURS PLAYERS

VIVIAN J. WOODWARD won 16 of his England caps while still a non-League player — and all 23 of them as an amateur (he claimed just 1s 6d (7½p) after one international trial match). He played with Chelmsford in the Southern League before joining Spurs and his 19 goals in 27 matches in 1908-09 helped Tottenham into the First Division. A slightly-built centre-forward, Woodward relied on skill and brains rather than brawn. He played 38 times for England at amateur level (winning Olympic gold medals in 1908 and 1912) and in his 23 Full Internationals he scored 29 goals. After playing just one season in the Football League with Spurs, he retired but came back with Chelsea the following year. In all, Woodward played 133 Football League matches and scored 50 goals. His last season was 1914-15 and he died in 1954.

JIMMY SEED was snapped up by Tottenham Hotspur after Sunderland gave him a free-transfer at the end of World War I. Seed had been gassed in the fighting and Sunderland must have thought that his career was finished. In fact, Seed went on to achieve great things with Spurs. The inside-right won five England caps and an FA Cup-winners medal when at White Hart Lane. He scored several vital goals as Spurs went on to win the 1921 FA Cup Final and in the second round of that season's competition it was Seed's brilliance that saw Spurs through a tough tie with Bradford City. Seed was first capped against Belgium in 1920-1 and played the last of his five games for England against Scotland at Hampden Park in January 1925. In 1927 he lost his place through injury, to Eugene O'Callaghan and Spurs caretaker manager Billy Minter surprisingly let him go to Sheffield Wednesday where he picked up his career to show Tottenham how wrong they were.

JIMMY DIMMOCK was a brilliant outside-left. Born within earshot of Tottenham's White Hart Lane, he scored the goal which gave Spurs the 1921 FA Cup — in only his second full season in the first team. At the age of 20 Dimmock had established himself in the Tottenham side and he played regularly until 1931-2, by which time he had scored 112 goals in the Football League and the FA Cup. Dimmock played three times for the full England team. He made his debut on 9 April 1921 in the 3-0 defeat by Scotland at Hampden Park and had to wait five years for another cap. On 1 March 1926 Dimmock played in the England side which lost 3-1 to Wales at Selhurst Park. In his third and final game for his country, on 24 May 1926, Dimmock finally got on a winning England side when they beat Belgium 5-3 in Antwerp, although the Spurs man failed to score a goal.

ARTHUR GRIMSDELL was one of the first Tottenham footballers to volunteer for World War I and, although wounded, he returned to lead the great Spurs side of the early 1920s. Grimsdell was a tireless wing-half and captain. He was even tried at centre-forward when Spurs were short of goal-scoring power but the move did not succeed. Nevertheless, Grimsdell was the inspiration of the team which won the Second Division championship and the FA Cup in successive seasons and even a broken leg in 1926 did not prevent him from returning to the side, although by then, both Grimsdell and the Tottenham team which had achieved so much, were beyond their best. Grimsdell won six England caps between 1919 and 1923 against Scotland, Wales and Ireland (with two appearances against each country).

RONNIE BURGESS joined Spurs before the outbreak of World War Two but had to wait seven years to make his mark in the team. Burgess skippered the great 'push and run' Tottenham Hotspur side of the 1950s. A brilliant wing-half, he was the first Welshman to be chosen to play for the Football League representative team and he was also chosen to play for the Great Britain team which beat the Rest of Europe 6-1 at Hampden Park in 1946-7. Burgess was capped 32 times for Wales, including a match against the Rest of the United Kingdom. In Spurs two title-winning seasons of 1949-50 and 1950-1, he played in 74 matches out of a possible 84. In 1954-55, as a reward for his loyal service to Spurs, the Tottenham Board of Directors allowed Burgess to join Swansea Town in his native Wales.

DANNY BLANCHFLOWER is probably the most famous of all Spurs' famous names. A cultured, articulate footballer, Blanchflower joined Spurs from Aston Villa in the 1954-5 season. Previously he had played with Glentoran in the Irish League and then Barnsley. Blanchflower wore the Spurs No 4 shirt with great distinction for ten seasons, captaining them to the 'double' of League and FA Cup, plus another FA Cup win in 1962 and the European Cup-winners Cup in 1963. He was voted Footballer of the Year in 1958 and 1961 and altogether played 553 League games for Spurs, scoring 27 goals. In 56 full internationals for his native Northern Ireland, Blanchflower scored twice and played in the 1958 World Cup finals in Sweden. A man with an uncanny ability to 'read' the game, coupled with accurate passing, Blanchflower was manager of Chelsea for a spell and also rejuvenated the Irish national team as their manager. For many years he has been a journalist, writing a widely-respected column in the *Sunday Express*.

TED DITCHBURN, like so many of his generation, missed seven years of League football because of World War II. Nevertheless, he played 418 matches in the League between 1946-7 and 1958-9, a run only ended by a broken finger suffered in a match against London rivals Chelsea. He won six full England caps, recovering from a shaky match in the 3-1 defeat at the hands of Sweden in Stockholm in 1949, to be recalled four years later for an international against the USA in New York. In 1956-7, Ditchburn enjoyed an Indian Summer when he won three more caps against Wales, Yugoslavia and Denmark. He finished his playing career under Malcolm Allison at Romford, but will always be remembered as the greatest exponent of coming off his line to thwart a breakaway forward.

ALF RAMSEY's transfer from Southampton to Spurs for the 1949-50 season was the last part of Arthur Rowe's 'push and run' jigsaw. Ramsey helped Spurs into the First Division and then on to take the League championship title the following season, as well as winning England caps, including three in the 1950 World Cup. A skilful and artistic full-back, Ramsey was also noted for his deadly penalty kicking, including a last-minute effort against the Rest of Europe in October 1953 which preserved England's unbeaten home record. Ramsey played in 226 League games for Spurs before he left in 1955, scored 32 goals and won 32 full England caps. He won fame as a manager by steering Ipswich to the First Division title and then England to the World Cup in 1966.

DAVE MACKAY's name is synonymous with guts and determination. Jimmy Greaves once said of him: 'Dave would run all day, tackle like a tank, shoot like a bullet, and he was one of the best first-time passers in the business.' Mackay joined Spurs from Hearts for £30,000 in March 1959. In between winning his many honours, he broke his leg twice — once at Old Trafford in December 1963 and then cruelly, in his reserve team comeback match. But the Scottish international wing-half fought back to win more honours. He was the perfect foil for Blanchflower in the great 'double' side; he won three FA Cup-winners medals with Tottenham; and when he left them in 1968 he began a new career under Brian Clough at Derby which earned him the joint-title of Footballer of the Year in 1969. Mackay played 541 League games with Hearts, Spurs, Derby and Swindon Town and was capped 22 times by Scotland.

JIMMY GREAVES was a goalscoring machine. From the moment he signed for Chelsea as a junior, Greaves maintained the uncanny knack of scoring on his debut for every team he played, from Chelsea's youngsters, through several grades of international appearances to his final club, West Ham. He moved from Chelsea to AC Milan in 1961-2 but his days in Italy were unhappy and that same season Spurs signed him for £99,999 — manager Bill Nicholson did not want him to become the first £100,000 player. Greaves played nine seasons with Spurs before joining his final League club, West Ham, in 1969-70 season. In those nine seasons he thrilled and graced the game with goals born out of sheer genius. Good players scored chances; great players, half-chances; Greaves seemed to score with no chance at all. In 517 League matches he scored 357 goals and in 57 full internationals, he found the net 44 times. It is a record which will surely never be beaten.

JOHN WHITE was one of the greatest inside-forwards of all-time, tragically killed by lightning on a golf course in July 1964. He joined Tottenham Hotspur from Falkirk in October 1959 and at his death he had played 183 League games in his five seasons at White Hart Lane scoring 41 goals. White also won 22 Scottish caps, scoring three goals and was a member of the Spurs 'double' side. He also played in the team which retained the FA Cup in 1962 and which won the European Cup-winners Cup in 1963. They called him the 'ghost' of the Tottenham side. Barely 5ft 8in tall, and weighing around 10 stone, White weaved intricate patterns around opposing defences with a style and skill rarely seen in the Football League. He missed only 17 games for Spurs during his career — they won only one of them.

PAT JENNINGS is an exceptional goalkeeper. Just as Greaves was a goalscoring machine, so Jennings seemed to be a goal-stopping machine. The Irishman from Newry, County Down, joined Tottenham Hotspur in 1964 after two seasons with Watford. When Spurs surprisingly let him go to Arsenal Jennings had played 472 League matches for the White Hart Lane club and it was almost unthinkable that he should cross North London to Spurs rivals in 1977. He fought hard to displace the veteran Bill Brown in the Tottenham side and became utterly dependable, saving his fair share of 'certain' goals to earn Tottenham many a point that might not otherwise have been theirs. In 1967 Jennings had the distinction of becoming the first Spurs goalkeeper to score a goal himself when the wind carried a long drop-kick into the Manchester United net in the Charity Shield match. Jennings played over 80 times for Northern Ireland.